ROUTLEDGE LIBRARY EDITIONS:
FREUD

Volume 4

PSYCHO-ANALYSIS

PSYCHO-ANALYSIS

A brief account of the Freudian theory

BARBARA LOW

Routledge
Taylor & Francis Group
LONDON AND NEW YORK

First published in 1920
Revised edition first published in 1923

This edition first published in 2014
by Routledge
27 Church Road, Hove BN3 2FA

Simultaneously published in the USA and Canada
by Routledge
711 Third Avenue, New York, NY 10017

Routledge is an imprint of the Taylor & Francis Group, an informa business

British Library Cataloguing in Publication Data
A catalogue record for this book is available from the British Library

ISBN: 978-0-415-83209-0 (Set)
eISBN: 978-1-315-85608-7 (Set)
ISBN: 978-0-415-71714-4 (Volume 4)
eISBN: 978-1-315-87148-6 (Volume 4)

Publisher's Note
The publisher has gone to great lengths to ensure the quality of this book but points out that some imperfections from the original may be apparent.

Disclaimer
The publisher has made every effort to trace copyright holders and would welcome correspondence from those they have been unable to trace.

MIX
Paper from responsible sources
FSC® C013604

Printed and bound by CPI Group (UK) Ltd, Croydon, CR0 4YY

PSYCHO-ANALYSIS

A BRIEF ACCOUNT OF THE FREUDIAN THEORY

SOME EARLY REVIEWS

"An admirable little outline of the theory and application of psycho-analysis . . . as a primer in the first elements of the subject, it could hardly be improved upon."—*Westminster Gazette.*

"Miss Low gives a clear exposition of the theories of Freud, and seeks to explain the nature of psycho-analysis. In a final chapter she describes the revolution which psycho-analysis must, she thinks, effect in the sphere of education."—*Times Educational Supplement.*

"An excellently written handbook . . . this cool little book, if the current controversialist can be induced to stop talking for a minute and read it, ought to help considerably to curtail this period of braying."—Rebecca West, in the *Star.*

"Every well-educated person of to-day should know something of the Freudian theory, and this book makes an admirable introduction to the subject, for it is short and clear, and requires no previous psychological knowledge on the part of the reader."—*Woman's Leader.*

"Miss Low's is the best elementary book yet published on psycho-analysis."—*Journal of Psychology.*

PSYCHO-ANALYSIS

A BRIEF ACCOUNT OF THE FREUDIAN THEORY

BY

BARBARA LOW, B.A.

MEMBER OF THE BRITISH PSYCHO-ANALYTICAL SOCIETY
FORMERLY TRAINING COLLEGE LECTURER

INTRODUCTION BY

ERNEST JONES, M.D., M.R.C.P. (LOND)

PRESIDENT OF THE BRITISH PSYCHO-ANALYTICAL SOCIETY
EDITOR OF THE "INTERNATIONAL JOURNAL OF MEDICAL PSYCHO-ANALYSIS"
AUTHOR OF "PAPERS ON PSYCHO-ANALYSIS"

LONDON: GEORGE ALLEN & UNWIN LTD.
RUSKIN HOUSE, 40 MUSEUM STREET, W.C. 1

First published . April 1920
Second Edition . October 1920
Reprinted . . . March 1921
Revised Edition . February 1923

Printed in Great Britain by
UNWIN BROTHERS, LIMITED, THE GRESHAM PRESS, LONDON AND WOKING

PREFACE

In addition to the deeper and more permanent sources of opposition to Psycho-Analysis, there have been two practical reasons why knowledge of it has spread slowly in England in particular. One of these has been the relative inaccessibility of the standard works on the subject, a difficulty which will soon be removed by the activity of the International Psycho-Analytical Press. The other has been the lack of any work giving a clear and simple account of the elements of the subject. This gap in the literature the present work is intended to fill. Miss Low is not the first to make the attempt, but she has the great advantage of having beforehand made an immediate study of the subject with the purpose of adequately qualifying herself for such a task.

Properly to appreciate Miss Low's success in accomplishing this task one should realize that it is one with peculiar difficulties. It is never an easy matter to present a complex science in outline, but with Psycho-Analysis several special circumstances make the task of simple and satisfactory exposition an almost insuperable one. To begin with, it is a new and growing science, and it is always found that the ease of popular presentation depends on the extent to which a given sphere of knowledge is relatively complete and finished. When fairly stable conclusions have been clearly defined from many angles it is possible to formulate them in simple language, even though the implications of them may be complex and elaborate enough. During the earlier stages of development, however, when the conclusions are more fluid and less sharply defined, it is very hard to reduce them to an easily intelligible form and to assimilate them to common knowledge, since the bearings of partial generalization are only evident to those who have already made some study of the subject. This is especially true when, as in the case of Psycho-Analysis, the conclusions reached are strange and startling; the more foreign they are to familiar knowledge, and the more repellent to preconceived opinions or prejudices, the harder it is to make them either acceptable or readily comprehensible.

That the deductions made from psycho-analytical investigations are both novel and not easily acceptable, Miss Low makes plain in her book, and she has not adopted the easier way of concealing these attributes of them. She has chosen the loftier aim of attempting to present all aspects of the psycho-analytical theory fairly and straightforwardly, and yet to bring them within reach of those who have made no previous study of the subject. I can answer for it that she has performed the first part of this task successfully, and can only hope that her readers will find she has performed the second part with equal success.

ERNEST JONES.

August 30, 1919.

FOREWORD

THE following brief outline of Psycho-Analysis is intended for those who are interested in this subject but cannot yet find time and opportunity to study at first hand the work of Freud and his followers, English and Continental.

Extreme condensation of a scientific theory both wide and deep is bound inevitably to create a certain disproportion and distortion of the facts involved. I am fully aware of this defect, but can only hope that the general presentation is approximately near the truth. If these pages can send readers later on to Freud himself, their purpose is fulfilled.

A word or two is necessary concerning the term " Psycho-Analysis." This is the name bestowed by Freud upon his own theory and practice: neither those workers who, starting from Freud's ideas as basis of research, have since developed on different lines, nor those who have incorporated other theories with the Freudian Psychology, are entitled to make use of the term. By so doing they create confusion, and obscure Freud's theory. They would do well to follow the example of Doctor Jung, of Zürich, who has invented for his own body of thought a new name —- Analytical Psychology. The Freudian theory and technique, and these alone, constitute Psycho-Analysis.

B. L.

August 1919.

NOTE TO THE SECOND EDITION

SINCE the publication of the First Edition numerous enquiries have been made concerning certain omissions in the List of Reference Books in the Appendix. I am glad to take this opportunity of explaining that the List is intended to include only those works which deal with the *Freudian* Theory and Practice, or its Applications; consequently some books bearing on this Theory, but diverging widely from it, have been omitted as inappropriate to my list. In this edition, however, will be found the names of the two most important works by Dr. Jung, who was originally associated with Freud's theories.

B. L.

August 1920.

CONTENTS

Contents

The common problem, yours, mine, everyone's,
Is not to fancy what were fair in life
Provided it could be—but, finding first
What may be, then find how to make it fair
Up to our means—a very different thing!
No abstract intellectual plan of life,
Quite irrespective of life's plainest laws,
But one, a man who is man and nothing more,
May lead within a world which (by your leave)
Is Rome or London—not Fool's Paradise.

Bishop Blougram's Apology (ROBERT BROWNING).

AN OUTLINE OF PSYCHO-ANALYSIS

CHAPTER I

THE SCOPE AND SIGNIFICANCE OF PSYCHO-ANALYSIS

Psycho-Analysis a Science—Its Subject-Matter—Its Nature and Method—Its ultimate Goal.

"It is the fate of all useful discoveries and improvements to meet with bigoted or interested opposition from those who would willingly remain in the beaten path of habit, rather than acknowledge any change to be profitable."

It is fortunate indeed that the above words cannot be applied in completeness to the new knowledge brought before the world of to-day by Professor Freud, but there is enough appropriateness in them to remind us that Psycho-Analysis has been, and probably for a long period still may be, face to face with a bitter struggle before men's minds are sufficiently understanding to render them willing to investigate it without prejudice. The reason for this is not far to seek. Freud himself has told us that his researches led him to one overwhelming certainty, namely, that the last thing man desires to know and understand is himself, and the words of Samuel Butler [*God the Known and God the Unknown*, p. 9], serve to show us a part of the secret. "Mankind has ever been ready to discuss matters in the inverse ratio of their importance, so that the more closely a question is felt to touch the heart of all of us, the more incumbent it is considered upon prudent people to profess that it does not exist, to frown it down, to tell it to hold its tongue, to maintain that it has long been finally settled so that there is now no question concerning it."

But this impulse to turn away from self-knowledge can, and in the interests of the individual's and society's happiness must, be overcome; for the help he has given towards such overcoming, a great debt of gratitude is owed to Freud. His work may be roughly described as the provision of new keys by which we can now unlock doors in the human personality hitherto impassable, through which doors we may pass into areas formerly unguessed at. By the use of the instruments he has forged, we shall in the future be able not only to prevent, to a very large extent, the creation of the neurotic and mentally diseased, but also to set the feet of the new generations on a more desirable path, leading to a destiny more splendid and satisfying than we yet dream of.

The task of Freud has been a hard and laborious one, fraught with difficulty and faced with every variety of opposition. There is neither space nor opportunity here to speak of the history of the Psycho-Analytic movement, a history of twenty years' work and struggle. Those interested can read for themselves Freud's own detailed account given in the English translation entitled *The History of the Psycho-Analytic Movement.*[1]

The results cannot yet be estimated: it is sufficient here to note that investigation and treatment on his lines is proceeding now in Europe, America, England, and his ideas have even begun to force their way into the strongholds of orthodox Psychology, Anthropology and Medicine. Already partial appli-

[1] Nervous and Mental Disease Monograph Series, No. 25

cation of the Freudian Psychology has been made in the treatment of "shell-shock" and general "war-shock" patients, under the ægis of the War Office itself. It would seem as though this new psychological knowledge and method will ultimately have to be reckoned along with the great epoch-making discoveries of the past—for instance, Newton's Theory of Gravitation, or the Darwinian theory, and may go further than these in the extent of its application. No doubt there will be extensions and modifications of the original theory in times to come, indeed Freud himself has already revised and modified some of his own theory. One might pause here to point out how big a testimony this last fact is to his mental power and sincerity; only the great minds are capable of adaptation and realization of fresh points of view, alongside with intense concentration and research on a scientific basis. A few lines, originally applied to another great creative mind, are appropriate enough to Freud:

He looked on naked Nature unashamed
And saw the Sphinx, now bestial, now divine,
In change and rechange; he nor praised nor blamed,
But drew her as he saw with fearless line.

Scope and Significance

Psycho-Analysis a Science.

I referred above to Freud's discoveries in comparison with some of the great scientific discoveries of the past, and the comparison certainly holds good in the respect that Psycho-Analysis belongs to the realm of Science, not to that of Philosophy, Metaphysics or Ethics. It is important to emphasize this fact, because critics, opponents and even supporters have been disposed to import into it implications and inferences which do not belong to Freud's own work. It may be allowable to argue that a Metaphysic is inherent in every scientific theory, but at least we are bound to accept Freud's own definition of his own work, namely, that his approach is scientific, that he has worked along scientific lines, and has tested all his conclusions by scientific methods, putting aside other considerations which may or may not be germane to the subject.

Since Freud began his work other explorers and investigators have come into the field and have brought new points of view, adding Philosophical and Ethical considerations; their conclusions may prove to be valid and valuable—only time can show—but this remains the special characteristic of Freud's view-point and method of investigation—it is established on an Empirical Scientific basis. He has looked at the manifestations of Mind, having first obtained an entry into realms hitherto unentered, and has followed out step by step the conclusions, using the most laborious and exhaustive processes to verify them.

There will always be many methods of arriving at the same—or more or less similar—goal; to some, Unconscious Mind and its workings has been revealed through the religious impulse and its influences; for others, intuitive impulses (the inspiration of Art in all its forms) do the same work; for others, the temperamental states of Mysticism bring illumination. We owe it to Freud that he has provided us with a systematic method which we can learn to understand, practise and test by accepted scientific laws, thus making available to large numbers the experiences which only the comparatively few could enter into through the channels instanced above; and even then experiences inexplicable and non-transmissible to others. But just because Psycho-Analysis is so strictly a science, employing only scientific methods (and a punctiliousness not always observable in the scientist), opposition has been raised. No preconceived theories, traditional or conventional standards, ethical considerations, or taboos, are allowed to influence the truth of the conclusions based upon phenomena observed and tested with exhaustive patience and judgment; that, at least, is Freud's ideal: in other words, a genuinely scientific ideal, but one difficult for most of us to tolerate. Schopenhauer has pointed out how the Philosophers and Scientists themselves are too often the worst sinners against sincerity; their fault is not that they are *unable* to see reality, but that they are *unwilling*, if that reality conflicts with their own beloved prejudices and desires. Therein, he says, they cease to be Scientists and Philosophers. Here are his own words:

"Almost all the errors and unutterable follies of which doctrines and philosophies are so full, seem to spring from a lack of probity. The truth was not found, not because it was unsought, but because the intention always was to find out again some preconceived opinion, or at least not to wound some favourite idea. . . .

"It is the courage of making a clean breast of it in face of every question that makes the Philosopher."

It takes time, and a great readjustment of ideas, before we can be grateful to those who pursue the truth with unrelenting single-mindedness, presenting her to us in her undisguised form. In addition, it must be realized that Psycho-Analysis has presented us with new material and a new sphere of operations. Before the work of Freud, truly "a voyager in uncharted seas," Psychology had scarcely any knowledge, even indirect, of the Unconscious Mind, and may be said to have taken no cognizance of it. If it be true—and none can doubt it—that "mankind has never a good ear for new music" (to quote Nietzsche's words), then it is understandable that only slowly and reluctantly can the new knowledge be appreciated, which probably is all to the good; time is needed for testing to the utmost extent the new theory, and for as wide an application as possible.

Not only has Freud revealed new material and new spheres of operation, the characteristic of all great scientific discovery; in addition he has made use of a new Method and Technique, employed by none before him, a weapon of his own forging without rules or traditions for its usage. Hence the great difficulty, in the beginning, of comprehending and following up his work. But now we begin to see that this new method has opened up boundless possibilities of research in the human mind, somewhat comparable to the possibilities revealed to the world by the Darwinian Theory, which one may say has become a part of the thinking-technique of man.

The Subject-Matter of Psycho-Analysis.

Any attempt to sum up the subject-matter of Freud's discovery must inevitably give a crude and very partially true statement, for it is impossible that so large a theme as a great scientific theory should be concentrated into a few phrases. This defect is, and inevitably must be, apparent in any presentation such as can be afforded in an outline of the present nature and scope: to counteract it, the reader who is genuinely interested in the subject must go to the fountain-head, to Freud's own work (a good deal of which is now translated into English from the original German) and to the work of his unequivocal followers.[1] For the present purpose, the subject-matter may be indicated as an *Investigation of the Content and Working*

[1] See Appendix for list of References.

of the Unconscious Mind and of the Relation between the Unconscious and Consciousness.

Before going further it is essential to realize Freud's use of the term "Unconscious Mind." To begin with its opposite. He signifies by "Consciousness" all the mental processes of which a person is aware, distinctly or vaguely at any given time, and in addition he employs the term "pre-conscious" for all that mind-stuff of which a person is not at the given moment aware, but which is capable of being (perhaps with certain effort) recalled.

But all that realm of mind which is unknown and is incapable of being spontaneously recalled by the subject, which is only made manifest (and only then in disguised form) in special states such as Dreams, Trances, Fantasies, Mania, etc., and can only be evoked by special methods, he terms the Unconscious.

This Unconscious, which term comprises both Memories and Processes, is in conflict with the tendencies and attitudes of the Conscious Mind (a further discussion of which will be carried out in a subsequent chapter), and it is this conflict with its bearings which is disclosed to us by the work of Psycho-Analysis. The exploration of the content of the Unconscious Mind and its processes led Freud to the formulation of his Theory of the Unconscious; the necessity for finding a Method whereby to explore, led to the creation of the Psycho-Analytic Technique, the latter, in fact, coming first and resulting in the subsequent theory. For Freud has not "evolved" any preconceived theory of the Unconscious. As already pointed out, it was through his attempts to study and cure abnormal and pathological mental states that he constructed his technique, and through the continued use of that technique came upon his great discoveries in the realm of the Unconscious.

The next step was to investigate the relationship between the Unconscious and Consciousness, which is all-important as far as the Therapeutic aspect of Freud's work goes—that aspect which must pre-eminently concern the practising doctor, the educationist, the social reformer, and the ordinary intelligent "layman."

If we pause for a moment to consider how comparatively small a fragment of mind is made manifest in the ordinary processes of life (though glimpses of a wider horizon may be obtained in the Art manifestations of great minds), we may realize what a new field for thought investigation has been thrown open merely by the established knowledge that there *is* Unconscious Mind—Mind continuously working without our conscious awareness and exercising influence of the profoundest kind upon our conscious selves. We have dimly sensed it here and there in vague manner; we talk of the artist's "inspiration," an unknown force coming from some unknown area of mind, working in non-understandable ways; we talk of the mysterious "Mob-impulses," of the "Herd-instinct," and so forth. Now for the first time we can follow up and trace out the workings of these forces. True, they may still remain to a large degree mysterious, as all life in its manifestations is, but our knowledge and power gain inestimably if we are enabled to guide, modify, and adapt those manifestations. In mediæval days leprosy was regarded as a miraculous gift from God before which men bowed their heads and folded their hands, with the result that thousands perished most horribly from this disease; to-day we may still regard its incidence as an unexplainable mystery, but we have enough knowledge to cope with it, to segregate the diseased, to limit its spread, to alleviate its ravages. So with the new knowledge that the realization of the Unconscious has wrought; we may never account for Mind and its processes, but we can now begin to explain and interpret a great deal hitherto wrapped in darkness, hence productive of disease and misery. More important still, even, we now can discover the *origins* of much in our conscious mental life, by which knowledge we may hope to shape the future more satisfactorily, adapting environment to the human being on more rational lines, and helping to transform mere blind following, or equally blind repudiation, of instinct into enlightened understanding. Enabled by the Psycho-Analytic discoveries to trace back to primitive forms and origins the complexities of the adult psyche, we begin to see far more clearly the value and validity (and the reverse) of our mind-stuff; we gain the mastery over it which knowledge brings; we can analyse and interpret it more correctly, and, above all, we learn to give to the Unconscious its share—a most unexpectedly large one—of significance and dynamic force. Consciousness ceases to usurp the whole stage of mental life: it learns to step aside to give place to the greater though less-seen actor in the Psychic Drama.

Nature and Method.

As has been already noted, the term "Psycho-Analysis" comprises both the Theory of Unconscious Mind (with its methods of working) and a Technique whereby that Unconscious Mind may be explored and interpreted.

The work of the Analyst is to note and follow up with the utmost care and exactness all the spontaneous manifestations and reactions of the Patient, physical and mental.

He must observe everything that is produced in talk; all the manifestations of which the Patient himself may be quite unaware (such as trifling physical habits, sudden bodily and facial movements, sighs, smiles, hesitation, and so forth); all his emotional reactions, all the material of night-dreams, day-dreams, fantasies. All these form the stuff out of which, by degrees, the Patient (under the guidance of the Analyst) makes a synthesis; thereby revealing to himself a "map" of his own psyche, and the springs of action and feeling which hitherto have lain, unknown and unknowable, in the Unconscious, manifest (if at all) to Consciousness, only in disguised and distorted aspect. One essential feature of the investigation is that it must be comprehensive. The ever-present selection and criticism of the conscious "intellectual" mind, absolutely necessary in certain spheres though it be, must be laid aside to allow free play to the spontaneous flow of all that emerges into the field of Consciousness. This is no easy task, above all for the highly educated sophisticated product of modern civilization. The impulse to select, to co-ordinate, to ignore irrelevancies, to rationalize, has become almost instinctive to most of us, and the first (sometimes the last) difficulty to be overcome often lies in this tendency.

Only by patient practice, by a strong desire to admit and reveal all the mental material, and a renunciation of the merely intellectual trends, can the spontaneous manifestations be obtained. Here the Analyst can give help and guidance; his function is to watch for the indications of any check on the free flow of spontaneous manifestations, to show the Patient when and how this is occurring, and persistently bring him back to the true line of investigation. In addition he must endeavour to create the atmosphere most favourable to the bringing forth of all the mental material. For it is not only the intellectual equipment but also the emotional development of the Patient which creates difficulties. Much of the mind content he *will* not bring out, because it is of a nature too painful or too incongruous to harmonize with his intellectual, ethical or social self at his present point of development. Fear, shame, modesty, self-love, all combine to make him suppress much of which he is conscious, and the duty of revealing it to another person becomes a most painful obligation. This difficulty can be in part overcome by the skilful and sympathetic handling of the Analyst; if he can instil into the Patient such confidence that the latter looks upon him as one to whom all intimacies may be entrusted; if he can impart something of the scientific attitude so that the Patient learns to look upon the investigation as not only a personal revelation, but, in addition, a search for further knowledge full of amazing interest and possibilities, then the difficult path may be to some extent smoothed. Difficult it must remain under whatever conditions, and it is well that all concerned with this matter, those especially who desire to know something of it at first hand, should realize that an Analysis involves trouble, patience, sincerity and effort on the part of the Patient or Enquirer no less than on that of the Analyst. The latter must be learner himself; he, no more than the Patient, can arrive at hasty conclusions of any validity; it is not for him to impose his own intellectual and moral judgments on the Patient; his part is to guide the investigation on the right lines, to illuminate, to compare and contrast, to break up complexities into simpler elements and, if need be, to interpret from his own stores of knowledge.

It has to be understood that far more is involved in the course of analysis than an intellectual process; the intellect must necessarily play its part, but far more fundamental is the emotional aspect. The emotional experiences of the Patient (both those which adhere to the revived memories and those which are the outcome of the Analytic process itself) create an instrument for further investigation, and ultimately bring about a new orientation. That which was previously unconscious only becomes present to consciousness through the channel of emotion, which emotion also serves to interpret the significance of the various psychic manifestations. Those who imagine that the Analysis consists in merely " talking over " the Patient's hitherto-buried mind-content, or in some form of confession, are mistaken ; the dynamic factor is the emotion which is tapped in order to be traced back to its original sources and again followed up in the fresh channels it has cut for itself in the course of the individual's development. The emotion is re-lived, actually re-experienced in the course of the Analysis. The difference between the process of "*talking over*" the mind-content and *experiencing* is the difference, as Freud himself has put it, between reading a dinner-menu and eating the actual dinner.

In a later chapter the Analytic process will be dealt with in further detail ; here it is enough if we realize that it is a process involving much time, laborious work and very continuous treatment. So far, the evidence of Freud and of other Psycho-Analytic experts seems to point to the necessity of a prolonged period for Analysis for extremely pronounced neuroses, to be shortened only at the risk of incomplete results. For slighter cases, and in the cases of the comparatively young, shorter treatment may suffice. If the necessity of lengthy treatment (with accompanying expense and sacrifice in various directions) appears a drawback, it should be remembered that all profound scientific research has always involved those same features—time, infinite patience, renunciation. We have accepted as a commonplace the fact that it took some centuries to elaborate the current Astronomical Theories, to establish the correct process of Blood-circulation, or even to ascertain the workings of the Anti-toxins. Need we complain if the investigation of that very subtle and complex thing, the Mind of Man, calls for many months at least of work and thought ?

Its Ultimate Goal.

What is the ultimate purpose and value of this new knowledge now available for man's use ? This is obviously an important question to put and to answer. To many it would seem as though its chief aim was the healing and restoring of those who are " abnormal "—the hysteric, the neurotic, the perverted. This indeed is one of its aims, an aim which so far has been achieved with striking success. The evidence supplied by Freud's own cases, with that of the various other practising Psycho-Analysts, gives proof of the power of this new scientific discovery to bring to what is called the "normal" level those who are seriously suffering in mind. We know that people who have for long years been troubled with nervous breakdown, violent obsessions, inability to work, numerous physical ills, supposed mania, shell-shock war cases—all these have been helped to a complete or very nearly complete "cure" (to make use of an unsatisfactory and somewhat misleading word), or, as one might express it, a new orientation towards life which renders them capable of adaptation to its necessities. There remains no longer any question as to this: we have at the present moment enough documentary and verbal evidence to form conclusions. In Vienna, in Zürich, in Berlin, in Holland, in England, in the United States, the work goes on continuously under trained experts, and year by year the evidence accumulates. Perhaps to no one, with the exception of the Patient, are the results so surprising as to the Analyst himself; none but he can realize the extent and force of the psychic conflict revealed before his eyes, consequently none but he can judge truly of the changes made. Yet in their cruder and more obvious forms the outside world too can note the changes; the throwing off of invalidism, the increased power of work and concentration, the capacity for sharing in social life and its interests, the capacity for forming satisfactory relationships (marriage, friendship, and so forth) which before may have been conspicuously lacking, the power of enduring and mastering the blows of external fate—all these things are observable as results of successful Psycho-Analytic treatment.

This, then, is one of the purposes of Psycho-Analysis, the restoration as far as may be of those who have been unable to adapt themselves to life's demands, and, if the treatment is successfully carried out, all would agree that it is an achievement of the highest importance. Freud himself has pointed out how increasingly manifest in modern civilized life are the Neurotic and the Hysteric; and the social reformer, the educationist, the medical man will subscribe to this view. It would seem as if the pressure of what is called Civilization has been too extreme, too rapid in its action; the "Sublimation" process (the term by which Freud denotes the diverting of the original energy connected with primitive impulses, especially the sexual instinct, into fresh directions) has perhaps asked too much and asked it too hastily, and the result has been an upset of balance, a conflict for the human being endeavouring to fulfil unconsciously and consciously this sublimation-process. If we can do anything to remedy the evils that have developed, so much the better. Better still if such evils can be *prevented*, and here we are brought to another aspect, another aim of Psycho-Analytic knowledge—namely, its work in the education and development of the human being.

What is it, from the most diverse standpoints of Philosophy, Morals, Religion, Aesthetics, Politics, mankind has always felt with such poignancy concerning the human mind? Surely it is the baffling mystery it presents. The Artist has expressed it again and again in his attempts to grasp and lay bare man's motive forces; the Philosopher and the Religious construct their systems because they desire to obtain some key to the mysteries; the Politician aims at using Society and Men in certain directions, and to that end seeks to comprehend the stuff he works with. In all these realms the workers are faced with constant failure, largely owing to limited and incorrect ideas, and in our own day there is a widespread desire to enlarge and correct our discoveries.

"We are beginning to see man not as the smooth, self-acting agent he pretends to be, but as he really is—a creature only dimly conscious of the various influences that mould his thought and action and blindly resisting with all the means at his command the forces that are making for a higher and fuller consciousness. . . . Future studies in this direction (i.e. in Psycho-Analysis) must give us the secret to the formation of opinion and belief, and the methods whereby these can be controlled."[1]

If, then, we are right in assuming the need and desire of man for more knowledge of the thing which most vitally concerns himself—his own mind—and if Psycho-Analysis can supply some of that further knowledge, it has established its claim upon our respect and attention. As to the application of that knowledge, there can be no limits. Accompanying the evolution of man we seem to see at least two marked characteristics—the growth of Complexity and of Conflict. Biology, Physiology, Psychology

[1] Ernest Jones: *Papers on Psycho-Analysis* (revised and enlarged edition, 1918), ch. ii. p. 15.

have traced out the development of the former; Art (in all its aspects), Philosophy and Religion, the latter.

To find some clear path through the network which Complexity and Conflict weave about the footsteps of man has ever been the instinctive desire of humanity, some reconciliation, or at least some *comprehension*, of the irreconcilable. Here Psycho-Analysis steps in, with a capacity for help that promises to transcend that of any other single science. It may be described as having for its ultimate goal *a further understanding and a further harmonizing of the various elements of psychic life,* working towards that goal, as has already been noted, by strictly scientific empirical methods. Its wide possibilities, the vast fields which lie before us for its application, will be touched upon in outline in a succeeding chapter.

CHAPTER II

MENTAL LIFE—UNCONSCIOUS AND CONSCIOUS

Two Aspects of a Unity—Nature of Unconscious and Conscious Mind—Perpetual Reaction of Forces—The work of the "Censor"—Manifestations of the Unconscious in Conscious Life.

One of the greatest services performed by Freud in his research has been to demonstrate irrefutably the unity and continuity of all mental life. No longer is it possible to divide Mind into "Faculties" in the old misleading way: psychic life is a continuity in the sense that at any given moment it is determined by all that has previously happened and all that is happening. Nothing is accidental in the psychic realm. "There is no 'chance' in the psychic world any more than in the physical," says Freud.

What look like unexpected accidental

happenings are not so in reality. The explanation is that so large a part of our psychic life remains, and operates, in the Unconscious that we are perforce unaware of it: we see only end-results which thus appear detached, incongruous, causeless. Hence, one of the first requisites for understanding Freud's theory is a grasp of this basic fact, namely, that the psyche is one entity, in whatever sphere it may operate; Unconscious and Conscious mind are but two aspects of this entity, both acting and reacting uninterruptedly throughout life. We must realize the nature of these two aspects of mind in order to follow the rest of the theory, and it will be well to begin with the more dynamic of the two, that is, with the Unconscious.

Nature of Unconscious and Conscious Mind.

Freud has described Unconscious Mind as consisting of all that realm of the Ego which is unknown and cannot be spontaneously recalled by the subject, which is made manifest (and then often in disguised form) only in special psychic conditions (such as dreams, trances, fantasies, mania) and can be evoked only by special methods. The term "Unconscious" is perhaps open to certain objections:

critics have contended that since we can only be aware of anything by means of consciousness, nothing we are aware of can be in any realm but that of the Conscious; hence the term "Unconscious Mind" becomes meaningless.

This objection is based on terms rather than on facts. We can all agree that certain realms of our psychic life, at any given moment, are obscurely, or dimly, or not at all, present to consciousness, though we may have means whereby to bring those realms into the fuller light; they are, at least relatively, in the Unconscious. Perhaps the simplest crude analogy we can draw is to liken the Unconscious to the air surrounding us which we do not see in visible form (though we experience its influence and activities), do not feel directly except under special circumstances, yet all the time it is knowable under given conditions and vitally affects our organism. Freud holds that this unconscious part or realm in the mind of each individual has once been present to the instinctive mind; from birth (possibly even before actual birth) every experience, inherited and other, is stored up in the Psyche, and *in its original shape.* "It is a striking peculiarity of Unconscious processes that they remain indestructible. In the Unconscious there is no ending, there is no past, there is no forgetting."[1] All these experiences, throughout our developing life, remain and, in addition, form all sorts of new combinations, with the result that the most complex psychic processes may and do take place without ever becoming part of our consciousness. The existence of this unconscious realm of mind must be in part attributed to the phenomenon which Freud has termed Repression, which will be dealt with in later pages, but for the moment it may merely be described, in passing, as that process by which a part of the individual's experience gets cut off from the mainstream of his Conscious mental life, and is swept out of Consciousness, or only emerges in some distorted form.

If we turn to consider a little further the nature of the Unconscious, we shall see how markedly its characteristics set it apart from the Conscious Mind. Its content is made up of "Primitive" Inherited Impulses and Desires: that is, of those Impulses and Desires which belong to the first stages of the individual's

[1] *The Interpretation of Dreams* (authorized translation by Brill, 3rd edition), G. Allen & Unwin, Ltd.

life, while he is still untouched or very little modified by the forces of civilization which act upon him both from within and without as he progresses through life. Just as the Folk-belief belongs to a humanity which has not yet been modified by the "civilization" of a later-evolved culture, so the "Unconscious" belongs to the Infant and Child-stage of the individual, both as regards content and mode of functioning.

It can readily be understood, therefore, that Feeling is the predominant factor in the Unconscious, and reactions are instinctive, uncontrolled by the checks and curbs which operate in conscious life after the infant stage is passed. It is fairly easy to realize this from the behaviour of mad people, or of people acting under the influence of some exceptional stress (emotion, a narcotic, intoxicating liquor); the "reasonable" self, as we say, is in abeyance, and feeling is the predominant and dynamic factor influencing their behaviour: in other words, they are, for the time being, motivated by the impulse from the Unconscious without the interference of the Conscious mind.

Freud's theory of Unconscious and Conscious Mind leads us back to his still more fundamental conception of the whole psychic system. His working hypothesis of mind-structure implies a creative force, a prime mover, which constantly impels all animate life, and gives the mental processes their dynamic nature—a conception which perhaps corresponds in some degree to Bergson's "élan vital," although the deductions the latter draws from his hypothesis differ widely from Freud's.

Accompanying every mental process is a varying amount of psychical energy which seeks discharge, and this discharge is experienced by the Ego as pleasure, gratification, or relief. This tendency of the psychical energy (or, as Freud terms it, the "affect") to seek discharge determines the flow of mental life, and it is this tendency which Freud expresses in terms of "wishes" or "desires." Thus our whole psychic life is made up of a series of impulses (or "wishes") which create ever new impulses, or combinations of impulses, of the utmost complexity.

Now all these impulses (or discharge of psychic energy) aim at the fulfilment of two great principles, upon which all our life is based—namely, the *Pleasure-Principle* and the *Reality-Principle* (Freud's own terminology). Concerning these two principles more will be said in a later chapter. Here it must suffice to note that the former, the Pleasure-Principle, manifests itself as the basic principle of the individual in his primitive instinctive stage, while still comparatively little modified by the external forces of civilization. It evaluates all experiences in accordance with the pleasure or pain produced in the Psyche itself, and is therefore purely subjective in its standard. "The Pleasure-Principle represents the primary original form of mental activity, and is characteristic of the earliest stages of human development, both in the Individual and the Race. It is, therefore, typically found in the mental life of the Infant, and to a less extent of the Savage. . . . Its main attribute is a never-ceasing demand for immediate gratification of various desires of a distinctly lowly order, and literally at any cost. It is thus exquisitely egocentric, selfish, personal, anti-social."[1]

It will not be necessary to elaborate, at present, the above description. The Infant demonstrates the existence of the Pleasure-Principle as the basic motive of his every action in a manner comparatively easy to observe: he is aware only of his own desires,

[1] *Papers on Psycho-Analysis*, Ernest Jones, p. 3.

and insistently demands their fulfilment in the shape of food, warmth, the mother's arms, or any object he sets his heart upon.

But it is not only in the Infant that we can see the Pleasure-Principle working, though in him, perhaps, it works with less disguise, naked and unashamed.

Primitive man recognizes it by the elaborate system of taboos he has set up to avert the consequences of his fierce, self-seeking impulses; so-called "civilized" man disguises and distorts, often with amazing ingenuity, that same Principle which motivates so much of his behaviour; but we have only to study our own Fantasies and Dreams, our self-regarding unreasonable emotions of jealousy, vanity, and so forth, our disinclination to recognize reality when unpleasing to us, to realize the presence and frequent domination of the Pleasure-Principle within us. The development of Civilization bearing with it cultural, ethical, religious and social influences, does much to modify and adapt the force of this Pleasure-Principle, but no amount of civilization can destroy it or its dynamic power. Directly (especially in the Unconscious) or indirectly (in disguised forms in Consciousness) it is always operating, cooperating with or antagonistic to the other great psychical principle which moves us—the Reality-Principle. Freud has described this principle as having for its function the adaptation of the organism to the exigencies of Reality—that is, of the world animate and inanimate which lies outside and around every individual. It is obvious that if the individual were incapable of acting upon the Reality-Principle, and that to a very large degree throughout life, he would also be unable to exist. He must recognize the superior force of sea, air, gravity, fire, wild animals, in order to maintain life; he must recognize the claims, needs, and superior force of his fellow-humans, even in the most primitive society or community. Thus much adaptation we all, perforce, accomplish; but the degree and perfection to which we carry out adaptation is infinitely varied, and it is in the development of still higher stages of adaptation that we undergo the difficulties and evolve the psychical conflicts which Freud has set to work to show and unravel to the world. The dominating factor in our Conscious life—the Rational life as we may call it—is not Feeling (which we saw holding the predominant place in the Unconscious) but Reason. This life of Reason which we are apt to look upon as the whole, or nearly the whole, of normal life is, as we have seen, a slow-developed creation in each individual, a result of the combination of inheritance and the reactions produced by the pressure of the external world—of the family, the community, religion, culture. That life (of Reason) is suited and adapted to the environment into which the new creature is born: it becomes consciously-realized and enables the human being to maintain himself in existence, bit by bit adapting and modifying the more elemental psyche, which, however, still remains, imperishable and potent. Thus arises that condition of a perpetual reaction of forces which creates the intra-psychical conflict.

Perpetual Reaction of Forces.

It has been seen that the primitive psyche in the human being must, perforce, seek its gratification in despite of the prohibitions and modifications which "Civilization" sets up. But since the more evolved psyche is also bent on the gratification of its desires, it is a question of struggle, now one set of impulses, now another operating, or, more often, a combination of both. For there is perpetual interchange between the various impulses: the Pleasure-Principle desires stimulate man and give rise to his more instinctive thought or action, thus preventing that nullification and emasculation of his more primitive self which otherwise might take place if the "rational" self were predominant. True, such a condition of affairs is unthinkable, since always in the Unconscious the primitive Psyche is dynamic and its potency is far greater than that of the "rational" self. At the same time that same primitive Psyche is perpetually undergoing change and modification from the reactions of Consciousness, so that it will, in course of time, manifest itself in conscious life in a form approaching nearer to the necessities imposed by the more civilized Psyche. As an illustration of this, we see how the dreams of the young child contain in crude, undisguised form the wishes which are unable to emerge into consciousness. For example, he dreams of killing and cutting up or fiendishly torturing the unpleasant nurse or the severe mother who exercises authority over him. The adult usually expresses his wish for the removal of some person disadvantageous to his own interests by dreaming so-

and-so is dead, or ill, or gone on a long journey. The demands which Civilization has set up —that he may not thirst to visit violence upon his brother man—are respected in the shaping of his dream, though, be it noted, at bottom the wish remains the same in substance as that of the more primitive child-dreamer.

The Repression process applied to Consciousness—a process perpetually at work—of necessity creates and colours much of the Unconscious. From his first beginnings the individual is experiencing repression of innumerable desires, which desires must take refuge in the Unconscious, making up that psychic stuff which emerges, at times, in his dreams, fantasies, passing thought and action. It would seem essential this should be so as part of the sublimation-process which works out man's evolution, and, at all events, it is clear that such a process must profoundly influence the manifestations of the primitive Unconscious—above all, where the repression is carried so far that there is no outlet at all in the Conscious life. The previous illustration may be again referred to: the child who is brought up on a system of no violence and no resistance—who is perpetually trained to think and feel that anger, the combative instinct and most other strong emotions, are reprehensible, who is convinced it is his solemn duty always to love his own family, who is prohibited from the use of any violent language (it is perhaps a pity that this last prohibition should be one of the basic rules of the otherwise admirable Boy Scout Organization) and anything in the way of lurid reading—such a child is extremely likely (provided he starts with a fairly normal temperament) to fashion an Unconscious in which all those instincts debarred from any healthy and natural manifestation will find expression with startling force.

A case very recently under my own observation illustrates this rather effectively: a very scholarly man of about fifty, of a sensitive, refined temperament, looked upon by himself and by some of his circle as perhaps a trifle feminine in his character, not very inclined to the average masculine pursuits and pleasures, and a good deal of an artist and dreamer, discovered (to his own intense surprise) that he frequently dreamed scenes in which he was indulging in violent and obscene language, or uttered such in talking in sleep. Just at this time his affairs had become rather critical, in that his professional career had dwindled to a large extent, and there were various important changes affecting his domestic life. It seemed that the Unconscious had the opportunity of manifesting itself, and then it was to be seen that the undue gentleness and the lack of the "coarser" and more vigorous elements which so markedly characterized his conscious life were compensated for in the Unconscious: the repressions which he had experienced in early life (and the further developments from them in later life) had caused an excessive amount to be thrust into the Unconscious (he recalled how his mother, to whom he was devoted, could not endure him, even as a tiny child of four or five, to make noises in her presence, such as drumming on the table with his spoon or kicking his heels), and that material had persisted in force and vigour instead of getting worked out in any conscious manifestation, as, for example, the schoolboy stage of slang, bad language, or vulgar joking.[1]

To take another illustration, it is common to find in the Unconscious the Father-image

[1] For a most interesting exposition on the Significance of Obscene Words, see *Contributions to Psycho-Analysis*, ch. iv. by Dr. S. Ferenczi (authorized translation, by Ernest Jones).

shaping itself as a terrific and avenging deity, even throughout adult life, if the conscious relation between father and son has been accompanied by much repression. If the father, very early in the child's existence, is the far-off, punitive authority, in whose presence there are all sorts of taboos, before whom there can be very little spontaneous manifestation, but to whom respect and affection is due, the Unconscious is very often found to create a Father-image compact of all the desired and desirable attributes which the child was ever seeking, to compensate for the reality. Possibly the conception of a Christ, dominated by Love, Tenderness, Forbearance, and an all-comprehending Understanding, is the Unconscious creation compensatory for the austere and avenging Father-deity of the earlier Jewish conception.

Just in the same manner as the Repressions in the Conscious influence the Unconscious, so there is ever at work the reverse process —the shaping and modifying of Consciousness by the Unconscious.

This, perhaps, is easier to realize than the former situation, if we once again recall Freud's fundamental idea concerning the stuff of mind.

The Unconscious is essentially Instinctive and Dynamic, and is ever impelled to fulfil its desires, which desires, in their crude form, must conflict with the "civilized" desires of man. There is, then, a battle-ground of opposing forces, and in the conflict the powerful Unconscious is bound to react upon, and at times to conquer, the civilized forces. Illustrations abound which are observable in each of ourselves; perhaps a most obvious, and at the same time most striking example is of the order treated by Freud, in such illuminating manner, in his *Psychopathology of Every-day Life.* The upwelling from the flow of the Unconscious does not always manifest itself direct, but may shape the Conscious in the form of hesitation, embarrassment, temporary forgetfulness. A few of the actual illustrations may be helpful. Here is a case of forgetting a name: one of Freud's patients was talking to him about a certain summer resort, and mentioned three inns he knew there. Freud allowed two of the inns in question but disputed the existence of any third, saying he had spent seven summers in the vicinity and knew more about the place than his patient possibly could. At last the patient recalled the name of the third inn, which name was verified, as " The Hochwartner." Then Freud " remembered " —admitted the third inn and its name, which he had seen and passed repeatedly for seven summers. Why, then, was the inn and its name " forgotten " ? He discovered by Self-Analysis that this name had a certain resemblance to a Vienna colleague, Frankl-Hochwart by name. The Unconscious in Freud resented the work and existence of this man : the latter was Freud's opponent and a possible danger. Such an attitude was unacceptable to Freud's Consciousness and gets repressed into the Unconscious ; any link, however faint, which might bring this painful and unacceptable idea into Consciousness must be ignored : hence the inn and its name, which would have served as such a link, must be " forgotten." Thus the Unconscious overruled Consciousness, even in the face of a strong, conscious desire to recall the name.

As an instance of the Unconscious working through a so-called " slip of the tongue," Freud gives us this case : a doctor, who had been treating a wealthy patient, now convalescent, began cheering her with the prospect of an expedition to the country very soon, and the pleasures she might look forward to, ending up with, "You will be able to have a very pleasant time if, as I hope, you will *not* soon be able to leave your bed."

Here the entirely unconscious, self-interested motive works through and creates the slip. In conscious attitude and behaviour he was the most zealous and disinterested of doctors, putting the patient's interest first, without thought of remuneration; but the desire to continue treating the wealthy patient, found only in the Unconscious, forces itself out.

An interesting "Concealing Memory," as revealing the Unconscious, is given in the following record:

A man of twenty-four always retained vividly this picture from the fifth year of his life: he was sitting on a stool in a summer-house by his aunt, who was teaching him his alphabet. He found difficulty in distinguishing the letter M from N, and begged the aunt to show him how to do so. His aunt called attention to the extra portion (one more stroke) in the letter M. Why did this apparently trivial incident remain more than a thousand others? The reason became clear when it was found that the memory of this picture served to cover a deeper desire—namely, a wish, in later years, to discover the difference between boy and girl, and through the medium of that same aunt. Further, when his desire was realized, he discovered that the boy (like the letter M) had one portion more than the girl (the N). The Unconscious reminded him of this desire (a memory of which in undisguised form would have been unacceptable to his adult mind) by recalling to Consciousness the harmless picture of the five-year-old at his alphabet lesson!

Thus we see perpetually the Unconscious is shaping our Conscious action: a man seeking a mate will all unknowingly be looking for traits, physical and mental, which reproduce some of the earliest impressions made upon him by a woman near and dear to him—his mother, nurse, or elder sister. Colouring, shape, voice, gestures—the significance of all these things to us in a personality—are to be traced to the forgotten impressions and desires which lie hidden in the Unconscious. All of us know the seemingly extraordinary tenacity (we call it perversity even) with which some individuals pursue their quest for some desired combination of circumstances (such as the ideal woman, the ideal spot to live in, the ideal house) unaware often of any very strong conscious desire, yet incapable of being satisfied without fulfilment of their unconscious desires.

In extreme cases, such as the case of the medium, the hypnotized subject, the madman, it is easy to see the Unconscious shaping the Conscious, influencing the subject to carry out actions which he is opposed to in Consciousness. These two great forces of the Unconscious and Consciousness may, as we have already seen, exist as conflicting elements, or may be harmonized into one coherent "Mind-stream."

It would appear to be a question of balance, and it is easily understandable that such balance is a complicated and precarious achievement in our human existence. That we so often fail to achieve it is only too obviously demonstrated by the phenomenon of the neurotic, the mental defective, the insane; that it is achievable to a very large and satisfactory extent is apparent in those human beings who are capable of using their powers and fulfilling their life-purposes with a large measure of happiness and efficiency; that it is on rare occasions very completely achieved is proved to the world by the great Artist and creative worker in any direction.

The artist and creator is he in whom are

welded together the two forces, so that when he produces "consciously," as we say, he is also producing far more than his Consciousness knows or can explain : inhibitions are removed, the Unconscious may speak, and the Conscious is free to accept, interpret, and use the knowledge (intellectual and emotional) thus obtained. Hence, the more profoundly this harmonizing process takes place, the further is the creative worker on the way to great fulfilment. If, in addition, he have mind-stuff of a great order, then we get those creations which are hall-marked as genius —at least by those whose own Unconscious is sufficiently free to recognize them—such creations as Shakespeare's "Hamlet" and "King Lear," as "The Brothers Karamazov" of Dostoieffsky, as Leonardo da Vinci's *Monna Lisa,* as Newton's *Theory of Gravitation,* as Wagner's Operas, as Freud's own *Theory of the Unconscious*—all these (to select only a few instances from the world's greatest phenomena) demonstrate to the highest degree the twin forces of the Unconscious and Consciousness working in harmonized combination. If and when man can understand more of this process of combination we may hope to produce, not work of genius (since that is an incalculable quantity), but at least far more of the individual's capacities and instinctive creative power.

Such reflection naturally leads on to a consideration of the conditions which so frequently cause a conflict-situation between the Unconscious and the Conscious, rather than a harmony. "A solution of the conflict between the repressing and repressed forces may be reached, however, whereby the energy of the latter is diverted to other aims, in much the same way as a conservation and transformation of energy takes place in the physical world. Upon the manner in which this is accomplished greatly depend the future development and mental harmony of the individual. When the transformation is in accord with the demands of external reality and conscious ideals, it represents an important gain for the progress of civilization and culture, an amount of energy being set free that is devoted to carrying out the work of fulfilling the needs of society."[1]

Freud has bestowed a name on this situation. He supposes that the constant endeavour of the individual to adapt himself to his

[1] Ernest Jones, *Papers on Psycho-Analysis*, Introduction, p. 4 (revised and enlarged edition, 1918).

psychic environment, and hence to oppose and suppress his more primitive Psyche, has resulted in the setting up of a barrier between the Unconscious and Consciousness—a barrier he has designated the "Censorship," since its function is to watch over and inhibit the manifestations of the more primitive Psyche, which latter are forbidden to emerge where too incompatible with the demands of Consciousness.

In the individual it is fairly easy, at least in reference to some phenomena, to watch the Censorship evolving. The infant and young child at first manifests no recognition of taboos, and the primitive desires may express themselves at will in action and speech.

Bit by bit a Censorship develops both from without (due to training, parental commands, education, etc.), and from within (due to its increasing "civilization" and psychic development), and the primitive desires begin to be repressed—a prison-house is created for them—and as the forces of civilization close in around the individual, so does the barrier or Censorship between the Unconscious and the Conscious grow stronger in potency and more extended in its sphere.

Nevertheless, stronger than the strongest Censorship, the Unconscious is perpetually "leaking" through, so that we can observe its actual manifestations in direct or indirect form, according to the psychic situation. It may manifest itself in direct form, as we have already seen, in such states as insanity, delirium, dream, trance; in the actions regarded as criminal—intense, uncontrollable, murderous anger, mysterious, intuitive cunning, obscene curiosity, unveiled exhibitionism; in the more normal "ordinary" life in all those actions which Freud has described to us in his *Psychopathology of Every-day Life*—slips of tongue and pen, absent-mindedness, confusions, unaccountable recognitions, seemingly sudden-acquired knowledge, "second-sight," and so forth.

These, as already indicated, are all *direct* manifestations of the Unconscious, though rarely recognized as such. The more subtle, complicated manifestations are to be found in the indirect forms, unrecognizable except by careful study and a knowledge of the technique and symbolism of the Unconscious. Indirect manifestations are to be seen in the form of Sublimation (Freud's term for certain psychic processes upon which more will be said), Narcissism, and all those Character-reactions which form a link between the two last-named.

In this chapter it is impossible to elaborate these various manifestations, whether direct or indirect, of the Unconscious. A little more concerning this will be touched upon in subsequent chapters, and a few illustrations now will suffice to demonstrate this force of the Unconscious in each of us, ever seeking escape from the Censorship; thwarted at times to the extent of becoming its fettered bond-slave; at times able to emerge in part only or in distorted and disguised form; at times so powerful that the Censor-barrier in all its strength is swept aside and the flood rushes through in its original torrential volume.

To begin with, the last type of manifestation—the markedly abnormal and pathological states—will give us best examples. In drunkenness, as is well known, the educated, cultured person may indulge in language (oaths and obscenities) and acts which he would certainly be incapable of in his normal condition. Here the intense interest and pleasure in such language (which itself is a "cover" for interest in the topics or ideas to which the language refers), strictly suppressed by the Censorship in the interests of civilization in Conscious life, bursts through, since Consciousness and its controls is suspended. This is a direct manifestation of the primitive interests still living on in the Unconscious.

Take the case of Lear, who is able to imagine and give vent to the most appalling and abnormal utterances towards his two eldest daughters when his "madness" has come upon him. Such ideas belong to his Unconscious and could not have emerged were he still acting under the control of the Censorship. Dostoieffsky's hero in "The Idiot" affords us a further illustration of the direct working in tremendous force of the Unconscious. His whole psychic existence is marked by the absence of the controlling-force of the Censorship, and he therefore speaks, acts, loves, without reference to the checks imposed by the civilization-forces. Accordingly, in the eyes of his fellow-men he is a madman, yet the Unconscious in each one at times responds to the appeal of the "Idiot's" Unconscious.

The smaller, seemingly trivial, "leakages" which nevertheless are just as symptomatic of the Unconscious, are dealt with at length by Freud in his *Psychopathology of Every-day*

Life, and again in his *Wit and its Relation to the Unconscious*. All who desire to understand more clearly must read these volumes for themselves. The instances already cited some pages back may give an idea of the material drawn upon (pp. 54–56).

As regards the indirect forms in which the primitive Unconscious manifests itself in Conscious life, perhaps one of the most interesting forms is Narcissism, the individual's love for and interest in himself and in all appertaining to that self. This Narcissism, so strong a motive in human action, is the evolved form of the primitive instincts of self-preservation and love of the infantile physical self—that is, the pleasure in the bodily movement, the feel of the skin, the functions, the appetites. All this becomes evolved into a more "civilized" self-interest in the adult which, however, still retains aspects reminiscent of the primitive attitude—vanity, egotism, exhibitionism, all modified to suit the demands of the strict Censorship.

The modifications, ever in process, lead us into the psychic condition Freud has termed Sublimation. This is the turning of the repressed sexual impulses away from their original object—namely, the Ego—to objects which subserve the social and cultural life of the Individual and Community, and in this way we are always experiencing indirectly the influence of the Unconscious. The primitive curiosity-instinct (originally a curiosity centred upon the body of the individual himself and of those around him) gets sublimated into the impulse for knowledge, study, scientific pursuits; the primitive cruelty-instinct gets turned into an impulse towards fighting, a skill in surgery, or a love of the chase; the primitive auto-erotism developes into interest in an object outside self, and thus developes into "normal" sex-impulse and activity, and from that stage again developes the sublimations of sex in the direction of art and all creative imagination. Again we see the Unconscious working in the character-reactions which bridge the gulf between the two sets of Narcissistic and Sublimating desires. Take such an illustration as a son's affectionate relationship to his mother. Here we have the Unconscious sex-impulse towards the mother, an expression of the more primitive Narcissistic self-love, in its desire for fulfilment and therefore pleasure, combining with a more sublimated development—the interest and tenderness for an object outside himself and a capacity for consideration towards that other object. The result in the fairly normal boy, say of seven or eight, will be a mingling of infantile impulse with the more "civilized" egotistic claims and wishes—hostility, tenderness, self-sacrifice, and so forth.

This child will, for example, seek to keep out strangers, to have his mother for himself alone, will evince jealousy of others who share her regard, will ignore much in her life and behaviour which does not affect his self, and at the same time manifest tenderness, self-sacrifice, and ideas often incompatible with reality—such as making his mother a queen, showering riches on her, dressing her always in silks, doing great deeds for her, and so forth. At puberty, when the individual's desire for sublimation becomes stronger and more urgent (though unconscious), it is easy to note the reactions set up from the conflict between the sublimating process and the demands of the Unconscious. The withdrawal into self (shyness, incompatibility of temper, love of solitude) is often the token of the narcissistic unconscious self demanding the interest and attention of the Universe, yet inhibited by the equally strong, sublimating desires for identification, for sacrifice, for admiration and appreciation from others. It is clear that the Censor-Barrier must be strengthened by the civilizing forces, and hence the more dynamic become the repressed Unconscious desires in their struggle against the ever-growing Censorship. Compare the child of the people with one of the highly educated and civilized class and we see that the former has, in certain directions, more opportunity for his Unconscious to manifest itself since there have been fewer restraining forces. In bodily affairs, in sex affairs, in expression of emotion, it is probably a recognized fact that the "uneducated" classes are hedged in by fewer inhibiting forces: they take sex more lightly, they make less of bodily functions (it is interesting to observe this in teaching different social types in schools or other institutions): they will give vent to emotion more unrestrainedly (contrast the gallery behaviour in a theatre with that of the stalls). Needless to say, every individual is influenced by the forces of civilization among which he lives, but they operate in very varying degrees. Contrast, again, the restraints to be found in art-forms in varying ages and conditions. Pagan art and literature, for example, has all its own restraints, but it is free from the restraint imposed by one of the great forces of civilization—namely, Christianity. The effect is obvious: in certain directions the Unconscious has become more and more dammed under this Censorship of Christianity, notably in matters affecting sex, and the result can be traced in the very different attitude manifested towards sex on the part of Pagan and Christian. This is but one instance as illustration; innumerable others can be adduced.

This chapter may be concluded with the following words of Freud: "A reaction from the over-estimation of the quality of consciousness becomes the indispensable preliminary condition for any correct insight into the behaviour of the psychic. In the words of Lipps,[1] the unconscious must be accepted as the general basis of the psychic life. The unconscious is the larger circle which includes within itself the smaller circle of the conscious; everything conscious has its preliminary step in the unconscious; whereas the unconscious may stop with this step and still claim full value as a psychic activity. Properly

[1] *The Conception of the Unconscious in Psychology*, Lipps.

speaking, the unconscious is the real psychic ; *its inner nature is just as unknown to us as the reality of the external world, and it is just as imperfectly reported to us through the data of consciousness as is the external world through the indications of our sensory organs.*" [1]

[1] Freud : *The Interpretation of Dreams*, ch. vii. p. 486, Authorized translation of third edition, with Introduction by Dr. Brill. (London : George Allen & Unwin, Ltd.)

CHAPTER III

REPRESSIONS

The Pleasure-Principle and the Reality-Principle—The Egocentric Impulses and Development of the Social Impulses—Conflict between the "Primitive" Impulses and the Restrictions imposed by Civilization—Creation of Repressions—Necessity for Sublimation—The Neurotic.

The Pleasure-Principle and the Reality-Principle. The Egocentric Impulses and the Social Impulses.

In the previous chapter it was noted that the Psyche was realized by Freud as the stage whereon is enacted the Intra-psychical Conflict between the more primitive and the more evolved human impulses. In the course of that conflict, and to serve its purpose, the Repressions are created.

It is necessary to return now to the discussion of the two great principles of Psychic life (already noted in Chapter II)—namely, the Pleasure-Principle and the Reality-Principle—in order to see how they operate in determining the psychic conflict.

It has been shown (see *supra*, p. 45) that the Pleasure-principle is the primitive human impulse, having feeling as its predominant motivating-factor. It is present at the beginning of life, and manifests itself strikingly and obviously in the infant-stages of the individual, in the physical, mental, and affective spheres. It is represented in the early, purely egocentric, impulses, which are perpetually seeking pleasure, the pleasure of nutrition, the sensation of many kinds of physical functioning, and so forth. It is clear that these egocentric impulses are essential to self-preservation and self-development, and that they must resist at all costs that which fails to subserve the ego's ends, that which brings pain and loss—lack of pleasure. But it is important to note in this connexion that so-called pain may subserve the individual's pleasure and passion by intensifying sensation; hence the egocentric impulses may be found seeking pain in order to turn it into a more intensified pleasure, such as the impulse seen in the newborn infant (and continued into adult life) to withhold the breath, the urine, the fæces for a certain period in order to obtain the maximum amount of pleasure from the ultimate discharge of tension. Here is the Pleasure-principle acting by the method of inflicting self-pain, and from this source we get the later development of Sadistic and Masochistic impulses. It is possible that deeper than the Pleasure-principle lies the Nirvana-principle, as one may call it—the desire of the newborn creature to return to that stage of omnipotence, where there are no non-fulfilled desires, in which it existed within the mother's womb. Freud has pointed out that Birth is no new beginning in the psychic life of the individual (any more than in his physical life), but rather an event which serves as an interruption to his ante-natal situation. It is an interruption terrific and painful in its intensity and suddenness, but one which cannot obliterate the individual's desire for the earlier situation, to which throughout life he seeks to return, and thus to revert to his beloved Omnipotence, once again free from all external and internal checks. Such a desire acts as a regressive tendency in humanity, giving rise to the conflict between the Static and the Dynamic ideals, typified again and again in Myth and Folklore, in such forms as the Atlas-story, the Golden Apples of the Hesperides, Thumbykin, Alice in Wonderland; all these express the desire for the first stages of life (and still more, ante-natal life) when one was the omnipotent, protected being, able to enjoy delightful egocentric pleasures, and, further, the desire never to leave that stage, never to grow old, nor face change and death.

"In our innermost soul we are still children, and we remain so throughout life," says Freud, to which we may add the saying quoted by Ferenczi, "Grattez l'adulte et vous y trouverez l'enfant," sayings which sum up what has just been noted—namely, our wish to maintain and conserve the primordial state, and the *persistence* of these egocentric impulses dominated by the Pleasure-principle which belong to that primordial situation. Side by side, however, with the Pleasure-principle we see operating the second great psychic principle—namely, the Reality-principle—and it is this which must next be considered.

As already stated, Freud holds that the Reality-principle has for its function the adaptation of the organism to the exigencies of reality, to "subordinate the imperious demand for immediate gratification, and to replace this by a more distant but more satisfactory and permanent one. It is thus influenced by Social, Ethical, Religious, Cultural, and other external considerations that are ignored by the earlier Pleasure-principle." [1]

But this Reality-principle, though the motive-force, seemingly, of so much in our adult and civilized behaviour, though guiding and controlling the Pleasure-principle in average normal human beings as regards conscious activities, can never abrogate the activity of the more primitive Pleasure-principle ; hence the intra-psychical conflict already referred to in the beginning of this chapter.

" The fate of the primary Pleasure-principle and the modifications it has to undergo before being allowed to manifest itself is one of the central objects of psycho-analytic study, which is thus the study of the fundamental driving force behind the majority of human activities and interests." [2]

The modifications referred to in the above quotation are essential owing to the evolution of those other impulses in man, often in

[1] *Papers on Psycho-Analysis*, Ernest Jones (Introduction, p. 3, revised and enlarged edition).

[2] *Papers on Psycho-Analysis*, Ernest Jones (Introduction, p. 4, revised and enlarged edition).

opposition to the primary egocentric impulses, although, of course, subserving the latter ultimately, but in an indirect and more subtle form. These are the social impulses which have led man beyond the wholly self-regarding stages.

Since man is bound to develop the other-than-self-regarding impulses, as well as the wholly egocentric ones, and since in any kind of community-life, under any form of civilization, he must live by the Reality-principle (as we have seen, life based solely on the Pleasure-principle is impossible except in a state of isolated oneness), it is obvious that he must adapt and change many of his most primitive desires to fit himself for existence. It is from this process of change and conflict, Freud has discovered, that the fundamental features of the Psyche are developed.

This process of modification and adaptation is a difficult and painful one; a long road has to be travelled by each human being before the Primitive mentality, dominated by the Pleasure-principle, can sufficiently change Impulses, Emotions, Methods of Thinking, so as to bring all these into line with the Civilization into which it is born. More difficult even than the sacrifice of the

Primitive Impulses is the getting free from the Primitive *Emotions* and *Modes of Thought,* for these latter may, and do, persist in conjunction with changed desires. The grown man does not cry for the moon, but he may cry for other objects, in the infantile mode, unable, just as is the infant, to adjust himself to Reality; the civilized man may have very largely outgrown the savage impulse to slay the person who is an obstacle to his own egocentric fulfilment, but the *Emotions* connected with such a person (Father, Elder Brother, Nurse, Teacher) may still live on in transferred disguised forms. Again, the primitive *Modes of Thought,* which must at all costs maintain the supremacy of the Ego, can easily live on, though applied to psychic experiences quite other than the early primitive ones. To the Infant, external reality is as nought, something to be ignored, as, for instance, when it shrieks for the glittering bright thing in the sky, unable to recognize the realities of space and substance. It is possible to maintain such a standard—the standard of egocentric valuation—and apply it to the situations of adult life. The failure, humiliation, sense of inferiority, to which most individuals are destined at least sometimes and in some degree by contact with the external world, can be re-acted to by the primitive method — that is, by ignoring the true situation and perpetually keeping the Ego the "top-dog" instead of employing a more adult method, namely, discovering the real part played by the Ego.

The Primitive Impulses, Feelings, Thought-modes, then, all persist, but in much changed, transformed and weakened forms, and this is due to what Freud has termed the process of *Repression*.

His theory of Repression lies at the root of his whole conception of mind, and thus is fundamental to any understanding of it.

From birth, according to his view, the primitive Impulses, Feelings, and Thought-modes are being perpetually "repressed" (that is, submerged partially or wholly) in favour of the new set of Impulses, Emotions, and Thought-modes, which are the products of the new creature's environment, external and internal. Repressed, it should be noted, but never wholly obliterated; the Primitive psychic life remains intact, but unable normally to emerge into Consciousness save in some transformed guise, such as in the Dream, the Nightmare, the Fantasy,

Bodily Affects, or in "abnormal" states, "Madness" and "Delirium." This primitive Mind-stuff is unacceptable to the Consciousness of the Individual moulded by cultural and ethical influences, but since it is imperishable (and here we have to note another basic principle of Freud's theory—namely, the indestructibility of psychic material), it must find a home outside Consciousness (and so takes refuge in the Unconscious and becomes "forgotten"), or, as an alternative, must so transform and disguise itself that it will become acceptable to Consciousness, since the latter will not recognize its true aspect and import.

Human Evolution would seem to have developed along the path of Sublimation, a result of the creation of manifold moral, religious, and cultural taboos, which latter give rise to conflict with the primitive impulses, pursuing the Pleasure-principle. Hence for each individual the human situation involves a process of Adjustment between the primitive and the more evolved, between the Pleasure-principle and the Reality-principle, a process, as can easily be seen, of most subtle complexity, fraught with every kind of difficulty, somewhat comparable with the process of biological adaptation. The fact that this adjustment-process is inevitable, in varying degree, to every human being, cannot remove the difficulties; to each newborn child will arise perils and problems in learning to suck, to exercise its physical functions, and later to talk, and so forth. Only in so far as the Sublimating-impulses prevail are these difficulties overcome; so it is in the psychic sphere. The primitive impulses have become modified and adapted through the power of the Sublimating-tendency, but this tendency is not necessarily always the conqueror even in Consciousness. Hence it is that Sublimation takes place in the case of individuals and peoples in an infinitely varying degree. There is the individual in whom the primitive egocentricity is sublimated to but small extent, so that he is unable to share in the Herd-activities, or adapt himself to social ends, remaining isolated and turned inwards (such as Jonathan Swift), with accompanying loss and gain. There is, equally, the nation which remains aloof, withdrawn, alien from and hostile to the influences of the Stranger-herd, of which type the Welsh nation is a good example. Without any possibility of the sublimating process, no evolution in the human psyche would take place, and we should remain at the level of Primitive Man, or the less primitive child; through its influence we get civilization, and its finest fruits. A great deal of Art is a Sublimation, Freud holds, of the primitive egocentric impulse "to see and be seen" and of the sexual impulse in general.

It follows that those primitive egocentric impulses must undergo change both in their nature and in regard to their valuation by the Psyche, and it is this process of change which creates what Freud has termed *Repression.*

If the Sublimation-process can afford an adequate outlet for the psychic energy accompanying the primitive desires, we achieve a fairly satisfactory adjustment. Take, for example, the young male's instinct for fighting: if this instinct can be gratified sufficiently in a sublimated manner, such as by organized boxing, wrestling, competition in games, and so forth, the instinct can continue to operate in a transformed guise without, possibly, too much dissatisfaction to the primitive Psyche. If a powerful Exhibitionist-instinct can obtain satisfaction through such a channel as the exercise of Public Speaking, Acting, prominence in some sphere of action, then again the original instinct in its crude form may cease to exercise itself in Consciousness, though always existent in the Unconscious. Here is the process of unconscious Repression at work, ceaselessly operating in every individual throughout life, a process of profound and complicated adjustments, involving both loss and gain. If we consider for a moment how easy it is and must be for such adjustments to go wrong, we realize that the Sublimation-process involving Repression is likely to be complex.

In the first place, the Civilizing-process both for the individual and for the race takes place with extreme rapidity. The human individual, in an incredibly short space of time, must emerge from his sensational existence, centering round his own ego, oblivious to the external world, into a social being, called upon to fulfil obligations imposed by the outside world in a thousand directions. His initial loves and hates, impulses and habits, must be cast aside to a large extent, or transformed out of recognition, to conform to the new claims put forth by his own psyche, and the demands of his fellow-humans. Added to this is the very prevalent "speeding-up" to their own cultural standards on the part of Parents, Nurses, Educators, and as a result, Repression is bound to happen, and too often in very excessive degree.

"This self-centred creature" (i.e. the infant), "urged by an inner and an outer compulsion, must, at least by school-age, grow into a large measure of self-dependence, self-control; must relinquish his claim to exclusive mother-care, relinquish absorption in his own charming body; must learn to check his fantasies by realities, and learn to plant himself as a separate, new individual. . . .

"From this babe, thus always in a condition of unstable equilibrium, and therefore exquisitely sensitive to injury, like all embryonic tissue, we too often demand a rigid standard of behaviour and feeling, applicable enough to the relatively stable adult."[1]

Here, then, is one obvious way by which Repression is produced.

In the second place, there are those human beings who by initial temperament are very unsuited to the particular environment into which they are born, and therefore have special difficulties to meet. Such types, for

[1] *The Conflicts in the Unconscious of the Child*, M. D. Eder and Edith Eder.

instance, as Lear, Othello, Becky Sharp (in fiction), Richard Burton, Swift, and a host of others, were probably all persons in an unsuitable environment, one which provided them with peculiar difficulties, and this circumstance, added to their own psychic constitution, failed to allow adequate outlet for the specially dynamic psychic energy accompanying their primitive desires.

Here, again, unconscious Repression probably to a very great extent is taking place, in proportion to the lack of satisfaction obtained by Sublimation.

We see, then, that in the case of both "average" and exceptional human types, the Repression process must inevitably act, carrying with it consequences that Freud has revealed to us.

In so far as the Sublimation-process does not fulfil the needs of the Psyche—that is, does not afford adequate outlet for the psychic energy accompanying the more primitive desires—other paths of discharge have to be created. The repressed impulses must find a way out, either in behaviour directly antagonistic to the Sublimated Conscious life (such as "Bad Habits," Violence, Criminality, and any Anti-social action), or in the form of

Psychoneuroses (such as Hysteria, Nervous Breakdown, Obsessional ideas, physical ailments, and so forth). In both sets of circumstances some part of the Psyche is being repressed, and the repression is not a sufficiently harmonized process.

Examples of such repression may be found accompanying us in every step of psychic development. Shakespeare has given us a splendid instance in "Macbeth," in the case cited by Dr. Ernest Jones[1]: he depicts Lady Macbeth, long after Duncan's murder has been accomplished, as characterized by a habit of rubbing her hands together, as though washing them. Here is the repressed wish coming out in the form of a neurotic symptom, a mechanical, apparently meaningless habit. Lady Macbeth desires to wash away the stain of guilt from her consciousness. The process of sublimation cannot be effectively achieved, either in the form of causing her to regard the murder as a worthy, justifiable action, or to take upon herself the consequences of her act. Hence she is in conflict and fear; she would suffer if she realized fully how much she desired to be free of her blood-guiltiness,

[1] *Papers on Psycho-Analysis*, p. 288, Ernest Jones (revised and enlarged edition).

therefore she does not realize it, but gratifies that desire by transferring her feeling to a "neutral" object. So she washes away imaginary stains from her hands, a mere "freak" which arouses no suspicion in herself.

With wonderful intuition the artistic genius leaps to the knowledge and conclusions that the Psycho-Analyst can reach only with painful toil; hence Shakespeare makes Lady Macbeth furnish a key to the riddle in her sleep, when the Psychic Censorship is relaxed, and the original wish, unrepressed by the Sublimating influences of Conscious life, can reveal itself. In her sleep-walking she cries out: "What, will these hands ne'er be clean? Here's *the smell of the blood still.*"

This is an illustration from the hand of the Artist, but we can as easily turn to real life for other examples. The attack of hysteria, the obsessional idea, "bad habits," bodily ailments developed without any apparent cause—all these are channels through which the repressed impulses struggle to get expression. Those who care to follow up the subject must turn to Freud's *Psychopathology of Every-day Life*, in which they will find a mine of information, and to *The Interpretation of Dreams.*

Such further illustration serves to show that the primitive impulses mostly concerned are the Sexual and the Self-regarding. It has to be realized that these two are the most dynamic, and are in addition just those which in every community-life, especially that of a highly-civilized type, are most unable to be gratified in anything like their original form and intensity. This non-gratification (or inadequate gratification) of the primitive egocentric Sexual impulses causes the profoundest complexes to form in the human Psyche; hence Freud's theory of the Complex is inevitably bound up with that of Repression. Briefly put, the "Complex" (a term first employed in this connexion by Dr. C. G. Jung, of Zürich) results from a damming of the psychic energy accompanying the profound primitive impulses, which remain undischarged owing to the checks imposed by the Sublimating-forces.

The emotions connected with this arrested psychic stream, unable to get discharged, become sources of pain to the psyche, and therefore the impulse, and all the feelings and ideas carried in association with it, have to be "shut off," or dissociated from consciousness; a "knot" in the strands of the emotional being is created, by means of which fresh entanglements are ever being formed. Thus the need for Repression leads to the creation of Complexes, and in their turn the Complexes give rise to ever fresh Repression. The commonest simple example is the "forgetting" of a name because that name is associated (in the Unconscious) with some painful psychic experience which has given rise to a Complex.

An illustration of such "forgetting" is given by Dr. Ernest Jones concerning a medical student who became acquainted with a nurse at his Hospital, and saw her daily in the course of work for about a year. Later, he became more intimate, but he often found great difficulty in recalling her surname when addressing letters to her, though he had, of course, originally always addressed her by her surname. Investigation brought to light the fact that her Christian name was the same as that of a girl he had jilted in earlier life, and also of another girl he had passionately loved in boyhood. This name he could not forget, but he desired to forget his two failures in love. He identified the three successive girls unconsciously, and thus remained true to his first love, in a sense. But he did not wish to be reminded of his faithlessness (i.e. that he had now transferred his affection), which would be recalled by the different *surname*. Hence he may remember the first name, but not the surname. These in the three cases in no way resembled each other. It will be obvious that if Freud's theory of the conflict between the primitive and the sublimating impulses holds good, with its accompanying Repression-process, the Complex-forming capacity must be inherent in the human Psyche, beginning with life itself, and continuing to act, unknown to consciousness, as an inhibitory force throughout life.

In proportion as successful Sublimation is effected, so the Complexes will be "resolved," but only at the cost of forgetfulness of a great deal of our psychic experience; indeed, Freud's view is that the almost complete Amnesia for our earliest experiences—say from birth till the age of three or four—is due to the necessity to sublimate and therefore "forget" many happenings unsuitable and painful for later life.

The recognition of this fact (namely, of the repression-process) is essential if we are to understand psychic development, and, so far as lies in our conscious power, guide the sublimating-process to harmonious ends. It is the lack of such recognition that produces unintelligent training of children, misdirected and futile educational systems, and states of society which hinder the development of the individual. It is not conceivable that mankind should exist and evolve without Repression, since Sublimation must continue to be a path from the egocentric to the social life, and a means of compensation for unfulfilled desires. In no situation, so far as man has yet travelled, has his achievement kept pace with his desire, and it would seem that the Psyche, ever impelled by the Pleasure-principle, evolves for itself this process as a method of enjoying, at least as hallucination, its primitive desires. The infant who is no longer allowed the stream of milk from the mother's breast will continue the sucking movements of its lips, obtaining enjoyment in the fantasy of sucking; the child prevented from indulging his primitive curiosity for seeing and touching his own body and that of another compensates by taking an interest and pleasure in the clothes which cover the body; the lover, such as a Dante, unable to obtain his mistress, compensates by enjoying her in a different way

—as an inspiration and an ideal. Without such possibilities of compensatory pleasure the Psyche would be forced to fall back upon the primitive pleasures again and again, and thus hinder the progress of human evolution.

Especially when we remember the source of the most dynamic pleasure—the Sexual source—do we realize how essential is the power of Sublimation. For the primitive impulses springing from this source are the ones, as has already been noted, which remain most ungratified in civilized society, hence, are those which call for the greatest degree of Sublimation.

Religious, Social, and Cultural influences have laid a peculiarly heavy ban upon the gratification of the primitive Narcissistic and Sexual impulses, above all, of the latter; yet they remain the most dynamic impulses in each human being, demanding expression in some form, and flowing over into every sphere of psychic life. As a result, it is in these spheres that Sublimation is most difficult and most essential, both for the sake of transforming those impulses to fit the social needs, and to compensate the Psyche for such transformation.

It has been pointed out by Freud that the Sublimation-process involves loss (forgetting of psychic life, weakening of primitive impulse, often substitution of the less dynamic for the more dynamic) as well as gain, and such loss inevitably accompanies the gain at every step. It is the situation occurring so often in Myth and Legend—the necessary sacrifice, at a birth, of either mother or child. Both cannot survive; the mother may consent to be sacrificed for the sake of the new creation which shall bring a higher type into the world (such is the situation in the Volsung Saga), and the loss is outweighed by the gain. But if the new individual is no further advanced in the scale of humanity, and has little or nothing to give the world, then the mother-sacrifice has been made in vain. So with Sublimation: the gain from it (both to the individual and the community) may outweigh the loss and suffering it involves or vice versâ. Freud holds that it is the business of Society and the Individual to endeavour to bring about a satisfactory balance in the process.

For a certain number of human beings this process is achieved fairly satisfactorily on the whole, with a balance of gain, the primitive trends developing into products more or less useful to the Individual himself and to Society.

Even for this number we see that there is room for tremendous advance in knowledge in order to render the process more effective and less wasteful. It is hardly credible that, with such further knowledge, human beings need continue to lose their way so often and so disastrously in the process of self-development, to allow useful gifts and powers to waste away, to suffer so much more than they enjoy.

Further, there are many who never attain to even the average level of Sublimation with ease and adequacy, such as the Neurotic and the so-called "Abnormal." In such types the process is accompanied by too great effort and expense. The primitive impulses cannot be harmonized with the demands of Civilization, often owing to the intensity and exceptionally dynamic quality of the former. As a result, the psychic conflict is intense, creating either manifestations directly antagonistic to Society (murderous impulses, incest impulses, and so forth), or neurotic symptoms which tend to destroy the individual himself. In certain neurotic types, Freud discovered, there is often a highly developed moral, religious, ethical, or social sense, and a strong Idealizing tendency; hence a greater conflict than in a less developed type. In such an individual the desire for sublimation is so strong that it is proportionately more painful for him to realize and give way to the primitive impulses, and the very attempt to repress the latter renders yet more unattainable the desired sublimation. Take, as illustration, some of the great Mediæval Ascetics, who, turning with ecstasy of joy to a religious life, found, to their amazement and horror, the primitive impulses for ever surging within them. Unable to recognize these for what they were, vainly attempting to repress such instincts, they found more and more difficult the path of sublimation (e.g. St. Augustine). In other neurotics there is to be found an inadequate capacity for Sublimation, so that this type is unable to achieve the standard imposed on him by the community in which he moves; he cannot develop sufficiently far away from his primitive impulses, which insist upon expression in some disguised form, such as Hysteria. Here we have largely a Conscious process; still more difficult is the process when it is a matter of Unconscious Sublimation. The child in whom has been sternly repressed, from the earliest stages, a very strong interest in its genital organs, may develop an abnormal amount of unconscious repulsion towards these organs and the bodily functions they fulfil, covering the ungratified primitive interest. Yet his accompanying *conscious* attitude, ethical and moral, may be one which tends to idealize the body. His conflict will be intense because he is seeking a very high standard of sublimation which can only be attained by the yet further repression of the already partially repressed (but powerfully dynamic) primitive impulses. "Our unknown Repressions lead us ever further in the path of Repression," says Ferenczi, and the truth of the saying seems indisputably proved. It is a commonplace that the human types most distinguished for Idealism and Morality are also often those in whom the psychic conflict is most marked, and the explanation lies in this difficulty of adjustment between very strong Primitive and Sublimating Impulses. In addition to this difficulty, Freud finds another arising from the too great degree to which civilization has sometimes carried Sublimation. His belief is that it can only be achieved in every age and community up to a certain standard, and if the claims of Civilization demand more than the possible amount, and that amount too quickly, then again a too great psychic conflict is set up, resulting in the Neurotic type.

He holds, for instance, that possibly sublimation of the sexual impulses has gone too far, and has produced Repressions too great to be dealt with successfully. In Western Europe, especially, sex-repression begins very early, either through the method of ignoring sex in the child, or by the heavy restraints laid upon the exercise or manifestation of the sex-function, except under certain specified conditions, and to this attitude, explicit and implicit, Freud attributes very many of the Neuroses which exist in modern civilized societies.

Here, and to conclude this chapter, a few words on Freud's sexual theory will be useful. That theory—namely, that all the primitive trends of the Psyche are sexual in origin—has created the greatest antagonism. Partly this may be due to the fact that such a view is new; partly to the fact demonstrated by Freud, that the strongest repressions are associated with the primitive sex-impulses. That which we do not desire to see does not exist for us; one recalls the "forgettings," the "absent-minded" acts familiar to us all. If civilized man has been unable to accept his own sexual impulses, it follows that he will also be unable to accept a theory which discovers those same impulses to him. " Our unknown Repressions lead us ever further in the path of Repression." In addition, the repudiation of the theory is to some extent influenced by a misunderstanding of Freud's use of the term " sexual " (though the reason for that " misunderstanding " lies, again, in the need for repression). He uses it, as well as in its recognized sense, to cover a far wider sphere than is usual, including under it functions and processes not generally considered as of sexual nature, owing to the fact that such processes and functions have not hitherto been traced to their basic origin. If we take the human relation which Freud holds to be of the most vital import to the individual development—namely, the relation between parent and child—his sexual theory can be illustrated. The special characteristics of the Parent-Child relationship have developed from mutual sexual impulses. It is obvious that the same primitive impulses which exist in all mankind must manifest themselves among members of the same blood ; we have proof of it in the Incest-taboos to be found amongst primitive peoples in some form or other. Freud has revealed how the Greek Myth known as the Œdipus Myth embodies the horror and fear which Incest inspired in Man, and what that horror and fear served to cover —namely, man's instinctive primitive desire towards Incest, which desire has had to be repressed and sublimated in the interests of Society.

The son loves his mother, the daughter loves her father, with a love which has the essential and characteristic features, in many aspects, of the love which is recognized as sexual love between adult members of opposite sexes. To the male child beginning life the mother is Woman; she stands for all that Female Sex can mean to him at this stage of existence, and since to Freud all psychic life is a unity, he is compelled to realize that this child-love is potentially the same in kind as the love of a later stage which we unanimously recognize as sex-love. It is so only in the degree to which the child has developed his sexual wishes and trends; but these latter, as Freud has discovered through abundant data, exist, in a modified form, from the very beginning of life. The yet little-repressed desire of the young child to investigate its mother's body as well as its own, its interest in her bodily functions, its wish for exclusive possession, its jealousy and excitement centering round the mother (or other individual in the mother's rôle)—these are all images—shadowy and half-evolved perhaps, yet recognizable—of the characteristics of adult sex-love. This love for the one parent—on the part of the son for the mother, on the part of the daughter for the father—produces hostility in the Unconscious (since such an emotion necessarily must be repressed from Consciousness as unsuitable) to the other parent, and a revolt against his or her authority. Here, then, we are furnished with the situation of the Œdipus or Electra Myth, a situation Freud finds existing in the Unconscious, from the first stages, throughout life, revealed to us only in disguised form in Consciousness. One such manifestation, very little disguised, is to be found in the fact that all our later loves and hates are the outcomes of our first love, that for our parents. In literal truth, *Nous revenons toujours à nos premières amours*, either by the channel of seeking (unconsciously) in later life the men and women who can give us again what we most loved in the parents, or by the attempt, owing to what may be called a deeper repression, to get right away from that early influence,

This psychic situation which originates from sexual impulses (the Œdipus-situation) exerts manifold influences in manifold directions on the development of the Psyche, to be traced in such manifestations as an extreme repugnance to all authority (from the initial hostility to, or defiance of, the father), or an over-docile, slavish disposition (from desire to placate the dreaded father), or a dread of other men (from the dread inspired by the father), or an inability to find a satisfactory mate (from the over-persistence of the Father and Mother image in the psychic life of the offspring). Hence, the Œdipus-situation common to us all may or may not give rise to difficult complexes, manifesting themselves as neurotic symptoms, according as repression and sublimation can or cannot be carried out in fairly-balanced adjustment. It is in this connexion that Freud affirms the need for a more understanding training, environment, ethical and social ideal in order to achieve such adjustment.

The previous pages have pointed out that in the Parent-Child situation Freud has indisputably discovered a sexual basis, a fact unknown and unknowable save through his researches into the Unconscious; equally he has found that same basis in our other most fundamental psychic situations and characteristics, hitherto unrecognized as sexual. There is space for one or two examples only. Curiosity, often manifested in so sublimated a form as scientific interest, thirst for general knowledge, or interest in exploration, originates as a primitive sexual impulse—that is, in the pleasure the child experiences for investigating first his own body, later the bodies of others. This desire to look, to touch, to know, so far as it has reference to bodily spheres, is usually sternly suppressed in very early stages of life (inevitably so, perhaps, in the interests of Sublimation), and passes over into a disguised form fairly adapted to the proprieties of adult civilized life, in the majority of so-called "normal" people. Curiosity, within bounds, is admissible; it is not regarded as a vice (its sexual origin having become disguised), nor quite as an admirable quality (since its sexual origin is realized in the Unconscious, and that realization produces a half-condemnatory view in consciousness). But in the cases where the primitive curiosity-impulse does not become thus transformed, it becomes Exhibitionism, with its accompanying "Peeping Tom" propensities, of which there is far more concealed and suppressed (often a process involving anguish) than respectable Society may care to recognize.

Two features are noteworthy in the criticism with which the theory has been met. First, that the repugnance of the critics, in many cases, appears to have prevented them from any impartial study either of Freud's own theory or of the facts upon which he bases that theory. Secondly, that this same repugnance towards the suggestion of a sexual origin to our fundamental activities would seem to imply a belief that the Sex-impulse is a thing taboo, in its nature unpleasing and unsuitable for fulfilling the Psyche's need. Neither of these attitudes seems quite worthy of an age which claims a large freedom from prejudice. Bacon's splendid maxim, "Alienum me nihil humanum," might be conveniently kept before our minds for a guide in this connexion, as also the words of Schopenhauer in his letter addressed to Goethe in the year 1815:[1]

"Almost all the errors and unutterable

[1] Quoted by Ferenczi, *Contributions to Psycho-Analysis*, ch. x., "Symbolism."

follies of which doctrines and philosophies are so full seem to spring from a lack of probity. The truth was not found . . . because the intention always was to find out instead some preconceived opinion or other, or at least not to wound some favourite idea, and with this aim in view subterfuges had to be employed. . . . Most of us carry in our hearts the Jocasta who begs Œdipus for God's sake not to enquire further; and we give way to her, and that is the reason why Philosophy stands where it does. It is the courage of making a clean breast of it in face of every question that makes the Philosopher. He must be like Sophocles' Œdipus, who, seeking enlightenment . . . pursues his indefatigable enquiry, even when he divines that appalling horror awaits him in the answer."

CHAPTER IV

THE RÔLE OF THE DREAM

The Dream as the direct Manifestation of the Unconscious—Night-dreams, Day-dreams, Fantasies—The "Censorship" working through the Dream—Resultant Dream-Mechanism—The Dream and its relation to Consciousness.

The Dream as the Direct Manifestation of the Unconscious.

"THE interpretation of dreams is the *Via Regia* to the knowledge of the Unconscious in mental life."

In these words Freud sums up the rôle of the Dream in psychic life, and shows us the importance of it for an understanding and interpretation of that part which we are apt to regard as all-important—our conscious psyche.

By means of this "royal road" we can travel from the Unconscious to the Conscious, or conversely, and discover *en route* the psychic events which take place in the process of fusion between the two conditions.

There are, as Freud has pointed out, other direct manifestations of the Unconscious, such as Hysteria, Obsession, Delirium, all of which he has studied; but since the Dream is a phenomenon common to all, even to the most "normal" type, since it is possible to collect a multitude of data connected with it, Freud has made use of the Dream to a very great extent—almost as the basis, perhaps one might say—for investigation of his Theory of the Unconscious.

The primary function of the Dream, says Freud, is to protect sleep by stilling the activity of unconscious psychic processes that otherwise would disturb it.

If we recall again the Repression-theory, we remember that such unconscious processes are perpetually in action, only prevented from entering Consciousness by the influence of the Censorship — "the sum-total of repressing inhibitions," as it has been described by Dr. Ernest Jones.

In sleep that Censorship is relaxed, allowing the unconscious wishes to take the field; but such wishes and the psychic conditions involved would be disturbing to the sleeper (since out of harmony with his conscious psychic life), hence he must either remain unaware of them (in the great majority of cases we " forget " our dreams on awaking), or remember them only as distortions so seemingly meaningless and fantastic that they can be dismissed from consciousness. " Dreams are but sea-foam " has been the general verdict of serious-minded men, says Freud.

It is obvious that the Dream is inseparably bound up with the Repression-theory; in the Dream Freud discovered the very same influences working which he had discovered in waking psychic life—that is, an expression of primitive psychic wishes in conflict with the sublimated impulses, the result of such conflict giving the Dream its content, shape, and expression.

The very fact of the universal " forgetting " of dreams confirms the existence of the Censorship. Freud has found reason to believe that dreaming more often than not accompanies sleep, in spite of the average person's impression that he rarely, or never, dreams; but for reasons already cited we must " forget " (that is, unconsciously repress) this dream-activity in order that our Unconscious shall not be a disturbing force.

Before going further, it is necessary to point out that the Day-dream, the Fantasy, and the Hallucination are all related to the Dream proper (the Night-dream) and bear many of the same psychic characteristics, and in functioning bring about the same result—namely, the gratification of unfulfilled wishes repressed into the Unconscious or pre-conscious owing to the unsuitability of such wishes for Consciousness. But in the Day-dream and the Fantasy we may note that the Censorship is less relaxed—the conscious mental inhibitions act in a greater degree, and as a result, some of the aspects of the Dream proper are lacking, or are much less manifest; for example, such features as Distortion, Displacement, Condensation, and so forth, which will be considered further on.

In the Reverie and Fantasy there will be far more of intellectual work (Freud has pointed out that in Dream-making proper the intellectual process is non-existent), and since there is less relaxation of the Censorship there will also be less affect experienced by the subject—that is, the emotion associated with the unconscious wishes will not have as free a flow, for the stream of the Unconscious itself is more dammed up. We are accustomed to exaggerated and extravagant trains of thought and feeling in a Day-dream, but we still remain in a sphere conformable to some extent with reality; the day-dreamer may with ease picture himself as Napoleon Bonaparte, world-emperor, but not as a wild animal, an aeroplane, or a Greek Temple—situations common and normal to a Dream proper. Equally with feeling; extreme or exaggerated emotion may express itself in the Fantasy or Day-dream, but it is emotion centred upon objects and thoughts akin to our waking life, not as in the Night-dream, on objects with which no emotion is associated in Consciousness—such, for instance, as horror inspired by a coal-scuttle, passionate love-feeling for one's own foot or hand, fear of a chair, and so forth.

Turning once more to the work of the Censorship in relation to the Dream, we find here the most intricate, baffling, and interesting problems of Dream-activity.

Freud finds the Dream-function is to express an unfulfilled egocentric wish, unfulfilled since it has had to be repressed from Consciousness. The Dream, therefore, is carrying out the activity of the Pleasure-principle, giving expression to that which would be pleasurable to the primitive Ego, but is incompatible with the Reality-principle. As we have seen, the

Censorship must interdict such manifestations of the Pleasure-principle, and fulfils its task in one of the two ways already mentioned —by means of complete repression (" forgetting " of dreams), and by means of some harmless disguise (the remembered dream is mere childish nonsense, of no significance).

It is in the creation of the disguise that we get the complicated Dream-mechanisms which Freud has revealed to us.

The Dream-Mechanism.

The first principle to be grasped in reference to the Dream-activity is that it consists of two groups of mental processes: the *Dream-thoughts,* constituting the " Latent content," and the *Dream-narrative* (as related by the Dreamer), constituting the " Manifest content," as Freud has termed it.

" It is essential to keep distinct these two groups of mental processes, for in the appreciation of the difference between them rests the whole explanation of the puzzling riddles of dreams. The latent content, or dream-thought, is a logical and integral part of the subject's mental life, and contains none of the incongruous absurdities and other peculiar features that characterize the manifest content of most dreams. This manifest content is to be regarded as an allegorical expression of the underlying dream-thoughts, or latent content."[1]

These two groups have their origin in the Unconscious and in Consciousness respectively, and the work of the Censorship consists in the effort to prevent the former group from evolving into the latter, as has already been noted.

The most striking and easily-observed feature of the Dream is its use of *Symbolism,* a characteristic of the primitive psyche. The symbolism of the Dream is concerned with two activities: it manifests itself in connexion with the Dream-thoughts (residing in the Unconscious), and it is an outcome of the work of the Censorship which renders symbolic forms necessary for the sake of disguise. It is impossible here to touch further upon the subject of Symbolism; readers who desire to study the subject should turn to the chapter entitled "The Dream Work" in *The Interpretation of Dreams*[2] and to "The Theory of Symbolism,"[3] by Dr. Ernest

[1] Ernest Jones, *Papers on Psycho-Analysis* (revised edition), ch. viii. p. 190.

[2] *The Interpretation of Dreams*, ch. vi. (3rd edition, translated by Brill). George Allen & Unwin, Ltd.

[3] *Papers on Psycho-Analysis*, ch. vii.

Jones, for a full account of symbolism in the Dream. It is the symbolic nature of the Dream which creates one of the greatest problems in realizing its true significance, especially since the symbols will, of necessity, be connected with, and form a cover for, those wishes and ideas of which the Dreamer is (and desires to be) least conscious. "A final means of expression of repressed material, one which lends itself to very general use on account of its especial suitability for disguising the Unconscious and adapting it (by compromise formalisms) to new contents of consciousness, is the Symbol. . . . It is a substitutive, perceptual replacement-expression for something hidden, with which it has evident characteristics in common or is coupled by internal associative connexions. Symbolization essentially belongs to the Unconscious, but in its function as a compromise, it in no way lacks conscious determining factors, which in varying degrees condition both the formation of symbols and the understanding of them."[1]

From this quotation it is clear that the same process which has rendered the symbolism necessary—viz. Repression—will also be that

[1] *Die Bedeutung der Psychoanalyse für die Geisteswissenschaften*, Rank & Sachs, 1913.

factor which renders the interpretation of the Symbol by the Dreamer an extremely difficult task. In addition, the process of Symbolism is carried out unconsciously, and the individual is quite unaware of the meaning of the Symbol he has employed, often unaware that he has employed a symbol at all. It has been pointed out by Dr. Ernest Jones that "the field of sexual symbolism is an astoundingly rich and varied one, and the vast majority of all symbols belong to this category. There are probably more symbols of the male organ itself than all other symbols put together." Thus the Dreamer who dreams of a snake or a dagger in no way consciously regards these objects as phallic symbols, and most frequently, until the Dream-analysis forces him thereto, is unwilling to accept that conclusion.

As a further complication, we have to note that in addition to the constant symbolism which belongs, says Freud, to unconscious thinking as a whole, and "is to be found in greater perfection in the folk-lore, in the myths, legends, and manners of speech, in the proverbial sayings and in the current witticisms of a nation than in its dreams,"[1]

[1] *The Interpretation of Dreams*, ch. v. p. 245 (3rd edition, trans. by Brill).

there is also the individual factor. Even though, as Dr. Ernest Jones points out, the part played by that factor is a modest one, and, as has just been stated, the vast mass of Symbolism belongs to mankind, not to the individual man, yet, Freud reminds us, it is necessary to remember the plasticity of psychic material.[1] "The Dreamer, owing to a peculiar set of recollections, may create for himself the right to use anything whatever as a sexual symbol, though it is not ordinarily used in that way." An illustration of this occurs to my mind in the case of one of my own patients: in one of his dreams the sexual act was symbolized by the picture of a sea-bird swooping from a cliff into the sea. Symbolism, then, is the main process through which the dream-thoughts become in disguised form the manifest-content, and thus is of paramount importance for the interpreting of those thoughts.

In addition, we see other very important mechanisms at work which must be recognized before the dreamer can realize the true significance of his dream.

These are, primarily, the processes of Condensation, Displacement, and Dramatization.

[1] Ibid., ch. v. p. 246.

Condensation is the term applied to that process by which various elements in the latent dream-thoughts are fused together, in the manifest content of the dream, so that the dream as it comes to consciousness may be condensed to a tenth, a twentieth, a hundredth part of its original extent—that is, as it was in the dreamer's Unconscious. Condensation may show itself in various directions: one figure in a dream may be built up by fusion of the traits of various persons—proportions, face, hair, colouring, voice, dress, each of these may belong to different personalities and be fused together to form a composite portrait in the dream; similarly with places, episodes, and names. Again, the condensation-process may operate by collecting and making prominent the characteristics common to several persons, ignoring the differentiating traits. Freud gives an illustration of both these forms of condensation from one of his own dreams, in which he turns his friend R. into his own Uncle Joseph, giving R. his own facial appearance, somewhat elongated (the Uncle had a long face), with a thick, surrounding, yellow beard (R. has a dark beard, the Uncle a blonde beard). Further, he turns the character of

R. into that of his Uncle Joseph by selecting a certain quality belonging to the latter and transferring it to the former—the quality of stupidity—the reason for which he ultimately discovered to be a wish to discredit his friend R.

This condensation-process accompanies every form of dreaming, and the reason for it (just as in the case of the other forms of dream-distortion) appears to be two-fold. In the first place, it is a mechanism by which similarity or identity between different elements in the Unconscious can be economically transferred to Consciousness (or the wish for such similarity or identity); secondly, it is a mechanism whereby the psychic censorship may be evaded, since the condensation serves to disguise the real state of affairs. In illustration of this is the case already quoted, where the Dreamer attaches to friend R. the beard of his Uncle Joseph, an insignificant feature of resemblance which prevents him from realizing (save by the aid of Analysis) that he is taking up the same attitude to his friend R. as that which he entertains towards his Uncle.

Displacement, like Condensation, acts as a powerful distorting mechanism. By Displacement Freud signifies that process by which psychic importance is transferred to a given element in the manifest content from quite different unrelated elements in the latent content. Thus it is that in most dreams analysis reveals little or no correspondence between the psychical intensity attached to certain elements in the dream, as related by the Dreamer, and the associated elements in the latent thought, and this holds good conversely. It is a familiar fact to all that in a Dream the most intense emotion may centre around some entirely trivial and indifferent element. Here is a simple illustration, taken from the dream of a woman: She dreamed she was in the Zoological Gardens, just going round the wild animals' cages. Although the doors were all open, she was entirely unconcerned at the lions, tigers, hippopotamuses, and the great beasts. Then she wandered into the open air again, and suddenly found herself standing, transfixed with horror ("I felt my face had turned ashen-grey with terror," were her own words), gazing at a tiny stick which was lying in her path. Here is feeling displaced into a seemingly indifferent object—a harmless twig, whereas objects which certainly would inspire terror in waking life—the uncaged fierce beasts—are not invested with any psychic effect. Analysis of the dream revealed that the significant idea in the latent content was associated with the phallic-symbol which the twig represented (the Dreamer had played a game in the garden with a small relative that day in which little twigs figured). The absence of feeling connected with the wild beasts served as a disguise for elements in the Unconscious which were represented by these creatures. She was peculiarly terrified in actuality by any hairy, shaggy animal, which represented to her, so the analysis discovered, crude sexuality, and her terror served to cover an intense interest in these animals' physical habits; the indifference in the manifest content led her to pass by this train of ideas, hence to avoid recognition of what was in the Unconscious.

Thus Displacement accounts for much of the bewildering, paradoxical, contradictory nature of the dream, as perceived by the Dreamer in its manifest form, and only when the Displacement effects are re-established, linked on to their associated ideas, can the true significance of the dream (that is, the force of the *latent* content) be realized.

The mechanism of Dramatization will be perhaps more familiar to most people than the other complicated Dream-processes already mentioned.

By this mechanism the latent content is given a visual form, a scene of action, sequence of time to represent relations of cause and effect, inversion of elements, to show contradiction and so forth.

The commonest form of the dream is that of visual pictures—the Dreamer is usually looking on at the dream enactments as a spectator surveys the stage. This process, named Regression by Freud, involves the turning of abstract mental processes into their primary perceptions, and is characteristic of Dreams which tend to assimilate in form to infantile psychic activity of a visual type.[1] Such Dramatization is an invariable accompaniment, then, of Dreaming, and Freud points out that this process is an important factor in the transformation from latent to manifest content.

"It is the regard for *presentability* (Darstellbarkeit) in the peculiar psychic material, that the dream makes use of—that is, fitness for representation, for the most part by means

[1] A full discussion of the subject will be found in ch. viii. of *Papers in Pscho-Analysis* (revised and enlarged edition), Ernest Jones.

of visual images. Among the various subordinate ideas associated with the essential dream-thoughts, that one will be preferred which permits of a visual representation, and the dream-activity does not hesitate promptly to recast the inflexible thought into another verbal form, even if it is a more unusual one, as long as this form makes Dramatization possible, and thus puts an end to the psychological distress caused by cramped thinking." [1]

Just as the mechanisms of Condensation and Displacement create manifold disguises, obscurities and entanglements, so does the Dramatizing activity conceal or complicate the latent thought of the Dream, and these three mechanisms, to which may be added another, termed by Freud Secondary Elaboration (a more conscious mental process), are the chief factors in what he has described as the "Dream-work," or Dream-making.

Some characteristics of this Dream-work have been touched upon, and the subject cannot here be entered into more deeply. The following extract will perhaps help to summarize what has already been said:

"We have, above all, to lay stress on the

[1] *The Interpretation of Dreams*, ch. vi., "The Dream Work" (3rd edition, trans. by Brill).

fact that in the formation of a dream no intellectual operation of any sort is carried out; the dream-making is concerned solely with translating into another form various underlying dream-thoughts that were previously in existence. No creative work whatever is carried out by the process of dream-making: it performs no act of decision, calculation, judgment, comparison, conclusion, or any kind of thought. . . . Any part of a dream that appears to indicate an intellectual operation has been taken bodily from the underlying latent content, either directly or in a distorted form; the same applies to speech phrases that may occur in a dream. Even some of the waking judgments passed on a dream belong to the latent content. To repeat, there is in the dream-making nothing but transformation of previously-formed mental processes. Dream-making proceeds by methods quite foreign to our waking mental life; it ignores obvious contradictions, makes use of highly strained analogies, and brings together widely-different ideas by means of the most superficial associations."[1]

[1] *Papers on Psycho-Analysis*, Ernest Jones, ch. viii.; "Freud's *Theory of Dreams*," pp. 204, 205 (revised and enlarged edition).

As we have seen, one of the most important purposes served by the various mechanisms mentioned—though not the only function, Freud points out—is to so disguise the latent dream-content that the Censorship may be evaded, and, as we have also seen, this evasion is necessary, since the latent dream-content represents always and only the imaginary fulfilment of an ungratified wish. And in this connexion we understand why, in addition to the obviously disguising-mechanisms, such processes in waking life as doubt, criticism, and forgetting (partial or total) of dreams, must play a part. All of them are necessary for aiding the Repression process by which the unfulfilled wish is prevented from coming to light—a process often so complete that the manifest dream, far from representing an unfulfilled wish, would seem to deal with its contrary—a desire against something, a fear, an objection. But analysis can always reveal this merely as the manifest content, beneath which, as we go still deeper, is found the wish-impulse, distorted into some other form.

In reference to this matter, Freud has carefully pointed out that the wish which is the motive-power of the dream is always a wish which exists in the *Unconscious*, or associated with an allied unconscious wish, since otherwise there would be no need for Repression.

An example or two will show the dream-mechanisms in action. The first dream is one related by Freud in *The Interpretation of Dreams*, taken from his own experience. It runs as follows: "Company; at table or *table d'hôte*. . . . Spinach is served. Mrs. E. L., sitting next to me, gives me her undivided attention, and places her hand familiarly upon my knee. In defence, I remove her hand. Then she says: 'But you have always had such beautiful eyes.' . . . I then distinctly see something like two eyes as a sketch or as the contour of a spectacle lens. . . ." Space prevents giving the complete analysis which Freud provides, but a portion may be selected to serve the present purpose. Condensation is to be found in high degree. The incident of sitting at *table d'hôte* beside Mrs. E. L., who places her hand upon his knee, recalls a whole series of episodes in the dreamer's life: one from a few weeks back, when he had a disagreement with his wife at a Tyrolese health-resort because the latter was too friendly at the *table d'hôte* dinner with some other visitors of whom he disapproved:

another from the days of his secret courtship, when his fiancée gave him a caress under the tablecloth: yet a third relates to a disagreement during courtship, which was important enough to separate the lovers for a whole day. These incidents, and several others which were recalled, have fused together to form the one situation in the dream. Secondly, we see Displacement operating. In the forefront of the manifest content is the situation of a woman making unsolicited advances to the dreamer, and she is the daughter of a man to whom in real life he owes money: in the underlying dream-idea the chief interest is centred in the wish expressed by the dreamer to enjoy disinterested love, which costs nothing. The dream in its manifest content has "displaced" the situation—the woman seeks from the man what, in reality, the man is seeking from a different source. The affect is linked up with an indifferent object—another illustration of Displacement. Mrs. E. L. who is but slightly known to the dreamer, and towards whom he has no emotional attitude, replaces his wife, and the emotional interest felt for the latter has been transferred to the former.

Dramatization is obvious: the dream forms

what may be called a little Drama, in which the Dreamer plays a rôle, and various abstract thoughts, various emotions, are represented in dramatic form. Such, for instance, as the criticism of his wife's conduct at the Tyrolese hotel, his attitude towards Mrs. E. L. and her father, his desire for disinterested love, and so forth. Lastly, we see Symbolism at work in the employment of the scene at table (symbolizing the courtship days), the serving of spinach (symbolizing childhood days, in which stage the dreamer had a great antipathy to this vegetable), the spectacle-lens (symbolizing a friend who is an eye-specialist), and the speech of Mrs. E. L.—" But you have always had such beautiful eyes "—which turned out to indicate the unfulfilled wish of the dreamer that people would do things for the sake of his *beaux yeux*—that he might get " something for nothing," as is said.

The second example is a dream given by a woman patient treated by myself. It runs as follows :—

I was a child of about nine, living in my old home with my family. It was mid-day. I was just returned from morning school to dinner, and standing on the doorstep waiting for my mother to open the door. I was full of dread and fear, it seemed, because the door was not opened, though I had no apparent reason for fear. Then my mother came to open the door, but she was dressed in a blue dress the colour of your own of yesterday (i.e. of the Analyst). She was tall and commanding, and her hair had turned quite dark (in reality, she was short, and at that period her hair was light brown). I remember rushing wildly past her, and that is all I know. Something else happened, I forget what; I think there seemed to be a pool of water in one of the rooms, but I ran by.

A full analysis is impossible, but it can be shown that here again Condensation, Displacement, Dramatization, Secondary Elaboration, are all at work.

The dread and fear in front of the unopened door is an element derived from two childish experiences: one which came to light was the incident of her standing in agitation outside her own front door after morning school because she desired to urinate and was in fear of being unable to retain her water any longer (an "accident" which her mother would regard as a great disgrace); the other experience, about a year or two later in her life, was that of having once met, on a dark evening, a drunken man near her home, who attempted to molest her (or so she believed), and from whom she rushed violently away to her own house and stood beating on the door to get in ; but no one was in, and she hid in the garden shed. Condensation takes the two memories, both sexual in a wide sense of the word, and fuses them together into a memory of a fear and terror and humiliation connected with bodily organs and functions, associated with her own house and door.

Condensation again is active in the picture of her mother, who also has traits real or imaginary of her Analyst. Analysis revealed that the Patient gave the Analyst the rôle of mother in many aspects, and desired to substitute the Analyst for her own mother. Hence by fusion of ideas and elements the real mother becomes in part the desired object, and wears her dress and hair. Displacement is easily seen in this dream. The emotions of fear and shame connected with the urination which she can no longer control and with the assault on her by the drunken man, are transferred from those experiences to the waiting outside the door, and to the opening of the door, partly to conceal where the true effect lies. The " pool inside a room " proved to be the memory of a childish accident in a passage outside a door, at her school.

Dramatization is obvious throughout, especially in the incident of " rushing wildly past her mother," which represents the extreme agitation and culmination of emotion she felt when the door had at last opened and she could obtain satisfaction for her physical need. Secondary Elaboration is illustrated in her waking criticism " Something else happened—I forget what." A deeper analysis brought to light that she had urinated then and there in the passage (to her mother's great indignation and disgust) as soon as the door was open, and this memory was suppressed by the Censorship, the conscious mental result being that there was " something else," nothing of importance worth remembering. Finally, analysis shows that there is a wish-fulfilment expressed in this dream—namely, the desire to be again the little child at home (and, in addition, to have the mother of one's own choice), and to indulge in the forbidden bodily pleasures of such a period, primitive pleasures bearing with them interests and excitements which now, in her adult " civilized " life, have become taboo, lost in the

Unconscious, yet remain still dynamic because never sufficiently gratified.

The relation of the Dream to conscious life has been a difficulty to many who have not grasped the whole implication of Freud's theory. It is clear that through the Dream the Unconscious wishes are revealed, and in so far (even if in no other way) the whole Psyche is made more intelligible. Moreover, it is from these Unconscious desires that we are acting in our waking life, and from the revelations of the Dream-material we are enabled to see how and in what directions Consciousness is being moulded and influenced. The conflicts and repressions will emerge in this way, and in emergence can be handled and interpreted: thus not only are the deepest sources of Consciousness revealed by means of the Dream, but further, an understanding and readjustment of the hitherto hidden psyche is made possible.

The Dream, Freud points out, always employs current psychic experience of the most significant import, and in many cases it is only through the dream that it can be truly evaluated. Freud writes: "I am compelled to contradict the assertion that our waking psychic life is not continued in the Dream, and that the Dream instead wastes psychic activity upon trifling subject-matter The opposite is true: what has occupied our minds during the day also dominates our dream-thoughts, and we take pains to dream only of such matters as have given us food for thought during the day."[1] Through the knowledge derived from his dreams the Dreamer may re-orientate himself: it may be he will yield to the Unconscious wishes some of the valuation which hitherto they have never obtained, and thus will achieve greater harmony in his Psyche; it may be he will realize, and in realization will be enabled to readjust, the strength of his still-childish desires; it may be that the more primitive impulses will henceforth blend with the more sublimated Consciousness. To conclude, in the words of Freud: "In any case, it is instructive to become familiar with the much raked-up soil from which our virtues proudly arise. For the complication of human character moving dynamically in all directions very rarely accommodates itself to adjustment through a simple alternative, as our antiquated moral philosophy would have it."

[1] *The Interpretation of Dreams*, ch. v. p. 147 (3rd edition, trans. by Brill).

CHAPTER V

TREATMENT BY PSYCHO-ANALYSIS

Aim of Treatment—Principal Factors and Technique in Treatment—The Rôle of the Analyst—The Share of the Patient.

Aim of Treatment.

To the majority of those who hear and know something of Psycho-Analysis, the aim and object of the whole matter would appear to be the cure or alleviation of the ills experienced by the so-called "abnormal" or neurotic person, and to a large extent this view is correct. Nevertheless, it is only a part of the truth, for the aim of the treatment is wider than any mere attempt to deal with, and cure, a specific mental disease. The neurotic (it is difficult at any time to draw a sharp dividing-line between neurotic and so-called normal) may and does benefit from this treatment, but if we sum up briefly the purpose of the Psycho-analytic knowledge and treatment, we should be near the mark in saying that its purpose is *to set free the Unconscious with a view to the discovery and comprehension of the Patient's buried Complexes.*

As has been pointed out in previous pages, every human being experiences in some degree Repression, and consequently is subject to Complexes, which are capable of producing psychic conflict. In a very large number of cases there is conflict sufficient to weaken and hamper the individual in his progress through life; in a smaller number the conflict is so intense that progress ceases and retrogression takes its place. If, then, the buried complexes can be discovered and comprehended, obviously there is gain, whether the situation is more or less urgent, for this discovery and comprehension yields results not only negative (such as the resolving of the neuroses), but also positive, enabling the individual to use his own personality and powers more effectively, and thus to obtain a greater fulfilment in life.

"Nothing can be loved and hated unless first we have knowledge of it," says Leonardo da Vinci; and until a man realizes and comprehends his own psyche, unconscious and conscious, he can scarcely have free play for his loves and hates, nor discover his proper orientation.

It will be fairly obvious to the reader after the short survey made in the previous pages—very incomplete and generalized though it be—that the process of Psycho-analytic treatment is a difficult and delicate one, dealing, as it must, with such subtle and complex phenomena as the psyche and its mechanisms.

Principal Factors and Technique in Treatment.

In this treatment certain factors are of outstanding importance, and must be appreciated in order to obtain some grasp of the matter.

In the first place, just as in the case of all other relationships which involve close and emotional contacts, to achieve a fruitful outcome of treatment, a "Rapport" between Patient and Analyst is all-important. Without it nothing can be effected, and the treatment is so much wasted effort on both sides. Through treatment a most intimate relationship is set up between Analyst and Patient, more so than exists in the relations, for instance, between the ordinary Physician and his patient, the Teacher and his pupil, the Lawyer and his client, or the Minister and his church-member. In all those relationships a close and deep intimacy may exist, but all of them fall short, in one aspect at least, of the Psycho-analytic situation, for in the latter, and in that situation alone, the Unconscious is revealed and the Analyst is in the position of knowing and understanding all those intimacies which the Patient himself learns for the first time under treatment, experiences which are unobtainable in any other way. The Analyst gains possession of a fund of material which is the key to his patient's most secret and intimate psychic experiences. Clearly, the reluctance to yield up those experiences, the impulse to conceal and distort them, the shrinking away from realization of his own Unconscious—and such tendencies are inherent in every individual—can only be overcome in proportion as the Patient can put trust in the Analyst. Needless to say, there must be confidence in the latter's integrity, and, in addition, in his power of dispassionate observation, in his intellectual capacity to realize and judge the given situation, and in his willingness to share the Patient's point of view. Such equipment, naturally, is always essential to the Scientist investigating in any sphere, but to the Psycho-analyst more must be added, if he is to achieve success. He needs a very wide and varied experience of life and thought, a power of quick intuitive insight, and a readiness to adjust himself to any and every view-point and feeling-attitude. It is hardly necessary to say that all these requisites are rarely to be found, in high degree, in any one person, but such endowment is to be aimed at. The very gifted personality is able, naturally, to enter into close rapport with his patient, of whatever type and temperament, far more successfully than the more average Analyst, but even the latter can achieve this to some extent if he realizes sympathetically what is essential.

Another most important factor in Treatment is adequate length of time, one difficult for many people to appreciate. It is common to us all to seek quick returns for our expenditure, with minimum loss: unlike Browning's Grammarian, who cried in scorn,

> Leave *now* for dogs and apes:
> Man has *forever*,

we demand that a cure shall happen while we wait; but such a demand must be sacrificed by those who intend to deal seriously with Psycho-analysis. It is perhaps not strange that people who will fairly willingly give up time and money for a "Rest-Cure" or a big Operation, express surprise that Psycho-analytic treatment should ask, as they complain, so much from them in these two respects, above all, in the matter of time. It is but a further proof of what has already been noted—namely, the non-recognition of the importance of the psyche, especially that part of it which is not directly manifest in conscious life. But serious consideration will show the importance of the time-element.

In the first place, the work of discovering the Unconscious, owing to Repression (and, in many instances, to the patient's unconscious desire *not* to be rid of his neurosis), is difficult and prolonged, hindered by the latter's deliberate intention to conceal, and still more by the resistances in the Unconscious. Even when discovery and realization have been to some extent achieved, the Unconscious may again and again lapse into the old situation, indicating that there are still unresolved elements to be faced, which involves further expenditure of time. Sometimes patients of the more highly-educated, more "civilized" type need a longer period of time than even the uneducated, more primitive person, and for the following reason. The discovery and realization of the Unconscious is not primarily an intellectual process, although the help furnished by the intellect is of great value (and here it is that the stupid, rather dull person may find very great difficulties in grasping the whole idea); on the contrary, it is primarily an emotional process, through which the Patient must realize in *feeling* the buried material, not merely *know* about it.

In regard to this Freud writes: "It is not the not-knowing in itself that is the pathogenic factor (not the mere fact of repressed material in the Unconscious causes the harm), but the foundation of the not-knowing in *internal resistances* which first of all brought about the not-knowing, and which maintain it. In the subduing of these resistances lies the therapeutic task."

And still more strikingly, in another place he says: "If the knowing about his unconscious thoughts were as important for the Patient as those who are inexperienced in Psycho-Analysis believe, then for a cure it should be sufficient for the Patient to listen to Lectures or read books. These measures, however, have just as much influence on the nervous sufferings as the distribution of menu-cards in time of famine has upon hunger."

The process of getting to " know about " the Unconscious is often speedy in the case of the intellectually alert and introspective type of patient, but, as the quotations above point out, this quick achievement may leave untouched the real problem ; that is to say, the resistances will remain until the Patient can re-live the emotional experiences which have built up those resistances. It is a commonplace that one of the easiest and most effective methods of preventing further enquiry into any matter (a method used consciously and deliberately by many Politicians and Diplomatists, among others) is to " know all about " it beforehand, to regard as settled and beyond discussion the question in hand. Such is the attitude, very frequently, of the Patient under Psycho-analytic treatment. The unconscious resistances tend to produce it in Consciousness, and the Patient may very rapidly declare that he quite understands the psychic situation and no further investigation is needed. In other words, he is fighting against the Psycho-analytic process, and the overcoming of his opposition, which is part of the therapeutic task, must necessarily take time. The importance of the time factor is understandable also if we bear in mind that the material to be explored (namely, the human psyche) is not only resistant, but highly complex and complicated—" a continuously intertwined and often very entangled network "—only to be explored by delicate subtle instruments.

Dream-Interpretation, Free Association, Transference, these are the chief methods whereby the Psycho-analytic treatment is carried out, and all of them demand a knowledge of special technique combined with a general understanding of mind-processes.

Dream-Interpretation, as has already been pointed out (see Chap. IV), is one of the chief ways of arriving at the Unconscious.

The Patient relates his dream of the previous night to the Analyst, straight through without interruption or criticism on the part of the latter ; very often, even with the first outline narrative, the Analyst can obtain clues to the meaning and significance of the dream, but he adopts a passive attitude, making no " guesses," only noting carefully the dream-material, the patient's own comments on it, any emotional reactions he displays, and any symptomatic actions, slips of tongue, or other leakages from the Unconscious, which may occur during the narration. At certain stages he may decide to call the narrator's attention to significant connexions between different remarks or different portions of the dream, connexions to which the Patient is blind owing to his internal resistances, but which should be obvious to the Analyst if his own Unconscious is free to act. Such interpolation by the Analyst probably will lead to further remarks and discussion from the Patient, which again will all be observed with care by the Analyst. The next stage is to take the Dream, portion by portion, using always the method of Free Association, itself another of the essential instruments in Psycho-analytic treatment.

A slight idea of the procedure may be obtained from a given Dream. The following was related by a Patient of mine the evening after he had dreamed:

"I am in a bus going to South London, probably to Brixton. I find D. inside the bus, sitting by another woman, older than herself, whose face I don't seem to see. D. and I talk. I ask her if she is settled down now, and she replies, Yes, she is. Then she asks me if I am married, and I say, No. Then dream ends."

In telling this short and (seemingly) simple dream, it was observable that the Patient was embarrassed and made nervous tattoos with foot and hand, at the same time smilingly affirming that it was a " dull, foolish dream, with nothing in it."

The Dream appears as just one small whole, one complete episode, and, following the dreamer's Free Associations, the following points emerged: First, his feeling of annoyance at finding D. in the bus with him. D. (concerning whom much had already passed between Patient and Analyst) was a woman, unmarried, with whom the Patient had been very much in love about three years ago. He had a friendship with her of three or four years' duration, somewhat stormy in character, and had frequently during this period thought of marrying her, or of having relations without marriage. He admired her greatly, regarded her as much above him, but was never sufficiently kindled by her, so that his intentions and plans all hung fire until the whole relationship was abruptly ended by the lady getting engaged to someone else, and shortly after he heard of her marriage.

He regarded this episode in his life as discreditable to himself, revealing him as a hesitating character, lacking in courage and strong sex-desire.

Hence the meeting in the Dream served to recall these feelings of self-reproach, and he spent a good deal of time discussing his stupidity and cowardice in this connexion, at the same time declaring that D. was partly in fault also.

From this, still by Free Association, he passed on to the matter of his destination in the Dream, which he supposed was Brixton, and he narrated the significance of that place in his life. He had, it turned out, various associations with Brixton, but the one of special importance to him which now emerged was connected with "an absurd and humiliating affair," as he put it, in which, as a youth, at a dinner-party, he had covered himself with confusion by eating his soup too hastily, finding it terrifically scalding, and being obliged to rush spluttering from the table.

The connexion between this episode and his relations with his lost lady was at first non-apparent to him, so he asserted: after a good deal of denial and manifestation of annoyance he realized it. He then passed on spontaneously to speak of D. herself, as she appeared in the Dream. He found her "far less attractive" than he had known her in life, "rather dowdy and undistinguished," and he was vexed that she seemed cheerful and content, answering, "Oh yes, quite," with obvious happiness, to his query as to whether she was settled down.

This next led on to his reflections about "settling down," getting married and making plans for future work.

The next matter that emerged was concerning the other woman in the bus.

He said: "I wonder who that other woman was. The curious thing is that, though I never spoke to her and haven't an idea what she looked like, it really seemed as if it was she I was interested in all the time instead of" (here he corrected himself, and substituted, "as well as") "D."

This led on to more speculation about the other older woman, ultimately bringing the Dreamer to the realization that this person was his own Analyst—a conclusion he came to quite spontaneously and with a good deal of reluctance.

From this point the Patient went deeper. By further Free Association he proceeded to his attitude towards his Analyst, from that to his attitude towards women about his own age whom he regarded as intellectual equals, from that to his feelings in the present and past towards his own mother—in this last connexion bringing to light one or two hitherto-forgotten early childish reminiscences.

There is not space to continue the Dream-analysis here, nor to show the various emotional reactions of the Patient and the deductions drawn by him from this dream, but the method of dealing with a Dream has been sketched. It is worth noting, referring once more to the Time-factor, that the above Dream, so short as to Manifest-content, took over a week to deal with (even to a limited extent), pursuing it consecutively each day in the Analysis-hour.

Reference has already been made to Free Association, the technique to which Freud has given so important a function in the process of revealing the Unconscious, and a few words must be given to this. To obtain his Free Associations, the Patient observes and relates in the order of their appearance all the thoughts, passing reflections, mental images (whether coherent or incoherent, relevant or seemingly wholly irrelevant) which travel through his mind during the Analysis-hour. He must suspend all intellectual work —selection, criticism, and so forth—and simply use himself as a receptacle to admit the incoming tide of thoughts, fancies, emotions, of any and every reaction, in short —a task in which he is left free by the Analyst.

This welter of psychic material is subjected to the closest inspection and investigation possible, and if Free Association is truly carried out, the Unconscious emerges and causal connexions between apparently irrelevant disconnected thoughts or images will be discovered. In this way, much that was non-understood or merely "senseless" receives a meaning and a value. As an illustration, the Dream already cited (p. 139) will serve. Free Association brought out, through a long series of images and ideas, the close and significant connexion between two apparently quite unconnected incidents—namely, the dreamer's meeting with his old love D. in a bus, and the taking of a journey to Brixton. Free Association revealed that a significant feature was common to both these happenings, in the shape of the personal humiliation of the dreamer, which factor linked the two incidents and caused the Dreamer to identify them and thus bring them into proximity. Again, the " meaningless " action of this same Dreamer—an interlacing of the fingers—of which he was quite aware but for which he had no explanation, was made plain by proving to be a symptomatic sexual act.

Judged intellectually, Free Association is a quite simple process, requiring little skill or effort on the part of the Patient; in point of fact, it is one of the most difficult processes to carry out, not on account of its own inherent difficulties, however, but owing to the Patient's resistances. Freud points out that the Patient will vigorously endeavour to prevent Analysis proper, either because he fears the revelation of the Unconscious, or because he clings, unconsciously, to his neurosis which in actuality fulfils his unconscious desires in some manner, little as he consciously realizes this. The resistances take many and varied forms: it may be that the Patient is unable to produce any Dreams or any Free Associations, complaining that he has nothing whatever in his mind to tell; it may be that he prevents Free Association by hostile criticism and argument against the Analyst;

or he may take an "intellectual" method of resistance by dispassionately and critically discussing all the material presented, keeping all emotional disturbing ideas in the background, often even unaware that he has any emotional reactions.

Analysis must overcome each and every kind of resistance, and for this, again, time is an essential factor.

In addition to time, patience and courage are required from the Patient, since the laying bare of the Unconscious, as has already been noted, is a process necessarily painful, the upshot of which may cause vital changes in his whole outlook and manner of life, and will certainly involve some degree of sacrifice to reality.

A previous quotation from Freud (see p. 136) impressed the fact that Psycho-analysis is not an intellectual process primarily, but rather one based on feeling, and this brings out the importance of the third great factor involved in treatment—namely, the factor of Transference. The following extract contains Freud's own definition of the process he has named Transference:

"During the course of Psycho-analysis the development of new symptoms, as a rule, ceases. The productivity of the neurosis, however, is far from being extinguished, but exercises itself in the creation of a peculiar sort of thought-formations, mostly unconscious, to which the name 'transferences' may be given. These transferences are re-impressions and reproductions of the emotions and fantasies that have to be awakened and brought into consciousness during the progress of the analysis, and are characterized by the replacement of a former person by the physician. To put it in another way: a whole series of earlier experiences are revived, not as past ones, but in the form of a current relation to the person of the physician."[1]

This displacement of feeling gives the key to the Patient's situation, since the neurosis itself is a form of displacement; that is, an emotional reaction, excessive, or inadequate, or in some way out of harmony with the current situation, caused by the identification of this current situation with an older one. The patient re-lives, in feelings directed towards the Analyst, many of his forgotten or hitherto unrecognized feelings towards persons who have been in intimate and significant relation to him (Father, Mother, Sister, Brother,

[1] Bruchstück, etc., s. 103, 104.

Nurse, etc.). Only through this evocation of feeling is it possible for the unrealized affects to come to light, to be studied, and finally to be adjusted to the Patient's psyche as a whole.

Again, to quote Freud.[1] He (the patient) applies to the person of the physician a great amount of tender emotion, often mixed with enmity, which has no foundation in any real relation, and must be derived in every respect from the old wish-fancies of the patient which have become unconscious. Every fragment of his emotive life, which can no longer be called back into memory, is accordingly lived over by the patient in his relations to the physician."

Without Transference no effective Analysis could take place, and no therapeutic work could be achieved. It offers an immense field for developing the Patient's realization of his Unconscious, and at the same time creates many subtle difficulties in the process of treatment, just as it does in all forms of treatment of the psycho-neuroses. In respect to this point Dr. Ernest Jones says[2]: "The transference, however, is not peculiar to Psycho-

1 "The Origin and Development of Psycho-Analysis," *American Journal of Psychology*, April 1910, p. 215.

2 *Papers on Psycho-Analysis* (revised and enlarged edition, 1918), ch. xviii. pp. 347, 348.

analysis. . . . The only difference in this respect between other forms of treatment and the psycho-analytic one is that the latter does not encourage blind transference and then allow it to last, but, on the contrary, makes the physician and the patient aware of what is happening, so that the process can be understood, controlled, and resolved."

And Freud reminds us that "the Psycho-analytic treatment does not create the transference, but simply uncovers it, as it does other hidden mental states."

Since the Patient must re-live so much of his feeling-life in relation to the Analyst, it is not surprising that a delicate and difficult situation is created, involving both in strain and stress, but it is this very situation which is so powerful an instrument in dealing with the resistances, and the deeper the Analysis goes, the more it must proceed *via* transferences. In Freud's estimate,[1] "It is undeniable that in his endeavour to emerge victorious over the transference phenomenon the psycho-analyst is faced with the greatest difficulties, but it should not be forgotten that it is just these difficulties that render us the invaluable

[1] Freud, "Zur Dynamik der Übertragung," *Zentralblatt für P. A. Jahrg*, ii. s. 171.

service of making the patient's buried and forgotten love-excitations current and manifest, for in the last resort no one can be vanquished *in absentia* or *in effigie*." The Transference may show itself in various aspects, as dominantly positive, negative, or (more usual) as a mixture of both.

In the case of a marked positive Transference (that is, one showing affects of love, affection, sympathy), the difficulty often arises that the patient is desirous of becoming too dependent upon the Analyst, demanding from the latter guidance, suggestion, authority, all which demands must be resisted. In such a case the patient may prolong the treatment (unaware as to what he is contriving) through unconscious and conscious desires for further intimacy with the Analyst, and through that intimacy for further gratification of old desires and fantasies.

In the case of negative Transference (manifested in hostility, jealousy, envy, and so forth) there is the difficult problem of dealing with the resistances which the Patient's antagonism turns to his own purposes (that is, of preventing the course of Analysis), and of guiding him to realize this negative attitude at its true value.

In whatever aspect Transference reveals itself, it necessarily creates emotional reactions in the Patient, often of a profound nature, which must be handled in the course of treatment—no easy task either for Patient or Analyst.

Here we are brought to the part played by the Analyst in the Psycho-analytic process, a matter which has been often misunderstood and misrepresented by critics of Freud's theory.

His is not the rôle of Hypnotist, Suggestionist, nor Father-Confessor, as has been thought and even maintained by superficial critics: his part, as Freud has definitely stated, is, first and foremost, *to direct the process of Self-discovery.* By means of the technique he puts the Patient on the right road for that discovery, and assists him to keep to the road and note what is to be observed as he travels along it, such observation often being impossible to the Patient, unaided, owing to his own resistances.

Further, since there exists (as has been pointed out in a former chapter) a symbolism by which the Unconscious expresses itself, the Analyst uses his special knowledge in helping the Patient to an interpretation of that symbolism, not ready-made, nor forced upon the latter, but rather in the shape of guiding principles, from which the Patient may deduce knowledge applicable to his own psyche. As example, the Analyst may acquaint the Patient with the fact of Dream-condensation, and it is for the latter to discover how condensation is acting in his own particular dream. Or the Analyst may inform him of certain symbols, uniform in significance among all peoples, and again it is for the Patient to find out whether his own use of a given symbol conforms to the general use or has an individual content.

Yet, further, the Analyst uses the influence which he obtains over the Patient to help the latter in overcoming his inner resistances with a view to reaching that final goal of the Analytic treatment already referred to—namely, the Patient's own discovery of self.

In addition to this, the Analyst's help is essential in aiding the synthesis of the various elements of the Patient's personality. From his own wider experience of minds and their various manifestations, from his objective standpoint, he can lead the Patient to weave the now disentangled threads into a new whole, and to see hitherto unknown relationships between various aspects of the psyche. In all these directions the Analyst's work lies, and such work is essential to effective Analysis. What he must not do is to assume any of the already-mentioned rôles of Teacher, Suggestionist, Ethical Adviser, and so forth. To do so is often a temptation, since such rôles are always attractive to man's vanity, especially to one whose own Unconscious is but very partially realized by himself. For this reason (in addition to other obvious ones) Freud lays down the absolute necessity of a complete analysis under an expert, for all those who seek to practise his Treatment and Technique.

Psycho-analytic treatment differs from all other therapeutic treatment not less in this respect than in numerous others, in that the Physician does not, as in the case of these other methods, purport to carry out the cure, nor lay down directions for his Patient, nor substitute his way of life for the latter's, nor furnish him with other and different principles of conduct. On the contrary, he seeks to make the Patient discover his own orientation, however much it may differ from his own ideals and theories.

"If the Physician goes beyond this aim and, assuming the position of a moralist, teacher, or guide, proffers a solution of the difficulty based on his own judgment and necessarily influenced by subjective factors, he thereby oversteps the limits of Psycho-analysis, mistakes its mode of operation, and stultifies its purpose." [1]

The burden of the Analyst is not small, and the same may be said of the Patient who experiences more difficulty in bearing it.

Psycho-analysis demands from the Patient a serious sacrifice of time, money, and most of his other current interests, since for the period of treatment everything else must rank as subservient. But such sacrifices are relatively small compared with the far greater one involved in the giving up of his inmost self and desires to observation and investigation. It will be realized, at least in part, from the former chapters how difficult and painful a process this may be, demanding patience, determination, honesty, and, above all, renunciation. For he must learn to turn from his fantasies, from his pleasurable childish desires, from his unconscious gratifications, and adapt himself to a world of reality; he must, in very truth, " put away childish things," which

[1] Ernest Jones: *Papers on Psycho-Analysis* (revised and enlarged edition, 1918), ch. xvii. p. 315.

constitutes, perhaps, for him and for all humanity, "the great refusal." But, as in the case of the mediæval Pope, it may be that the refusal reshapes itself before his eyes into acceptance, bringing with it a new orientation in the form of a greater inner control, an insight into his own psyche and that of others, and, finally, a power of finding and facing reality.

CHAPTER VI

PROBABLE SOCIAL AND EDUCATIONAL RESULTS

A Revaluation of Values—Influence on the Community and on the Social System—Modification in Family-Relations—Greater Individual Freedom—Effect on Educational Ideals and Methods.

"PRAGMATISM represents a perfectly familiar attitude in philosophy, the empiricist attitude. A pragmatist turns his back resolutely and once for all upon a lot of inveterate habits dear to professional philosophers. He turns away from abstraction and insufficiency, from verbal solutions, from bad *a priori* reasons, from fixed principles, closed systems and pretended absolutes and origins. . . . Against rationalism as a pretension and a method pragmatism is fully armed and militant. . . . No particular results then, so far, but only an attitude of orientation, is what the pragmatic method means. *The attitude of looking away from first things—principles, 'categories,' supposed necessities, and of looking towards last things—fruits, consequences, facts."* [1]

The above quotation, if we substitute for Pragmatism the word Psycho-analysis, might stand as a description of Freud's theory, at least so far as its basis and general attitude is concerned. It is because the Psycho-analytic theory, working empirically, has looked forward to "fruits, consequences, facts," and found these latter in such abundance that its validity holds good, leaving aside for the moment the question of its agreement with many other already-known scientific theories.

We may look upon the Psycho-analytic theory in two ways: as an instrument-idea by which we are enabled to get into more satisfactory relation with other parts of our experience (the test of the "truth" of any idea, according to William James); and as a revealer of new knowledge, which creates manifold results for humanity in the direction of the Educational, Industrial, and Social System, Individual destiny, Family relations, arising from a revaluation of current values.

In the very limited space now at my disposal I can do no more than indicate a few

[1] William James: *What Pragmatism Means.*

of the far-reaching results which seem likely to come about from an understanding and application of Freud's theory, results which must not be hoped for without reckoning with opposition and hostility, since, as one philosopher has put it, "By far the most usual way of handling phenomena so novel that they would make for a serious rearrangement of our preconceptions is to ignore them altogether, or to abuse those who bear witness to them."

To begin with one of the most fundamental consequences, the application of Freudian Psychology is bound inevitably to produce, in Nietzsche's phrase, "a transvaluation of values."

A Revaluation of Values.

The primitive impulses, admitted and understood as the dynamic basis of our psychic life, bearing their own validity and splendour, essential to any harmonized consciousness, will obtain much larger consideration. The "rational" conscious life will be realized as part only of the whole psyche, not necessarily, nor always, as sole leader and guide. A social system must, perforce, be evolved which allows some satisfactory measure of freedom to the primitive instincts, alongside with Sublimation, and the undue exaltation of the ultra-civilized ideals will cease. This new ideal brings in its train revolution in our methods of Child-training and Education, which hitherto have dealt almost exclusively with Consciousness. From such an altered educational system we may expect individuals more capable of understanding, and more able to recognize intuitively, human motives, so that we may become less baffled, less foolish, in the face of certain human manifestations, such as Wars, Class Hatreds, Social and Religious movements, our "rational" solutions for which are almost always complete failures.

"One half of the Philosophers ignore the greatness of man, and the other half ignore his baseness," wrote Pascal, and it is this ignorance, in either direction, that Psycho-Analysis will help to remedy.

Inhibitions, external and internal, will not be estimated as the whole individual, but rather as a covering mask for what lies deeper. "No man lives in the external truth, among salts and acids, but in the warm phantasmagoric chamber of his brain, with the painted windows and the storied wall," says Robert

Louis Stevenson; and it is necessary that we learn the nature and force of the "phantasmagoric chamber" of our psyche, and attain to some measure of reconciliation between it and our "rational self." As Freud has summed it up: "A reaction from the over-estimation of the quality of consciousness becomes the indispensable preliminary condition for any correct insight into the behaviour of the psychic. In the words of Lipps, the unconscious must be accepted as the general basis of the psychic life."

Influence in the Community and Social System.

For the Individual, then, we may hope for a better self-understanding (hence for more internal harmony), for more opportunity to live from his deeper rather than his superficial impulses, and for more psychic energy to subserve his own and the Community's purposes, since, his inhibitions being greatly lessened, he will have that energy liberated for other ends. In addition, greater external freedom may be his through the changed attitude of the Community and the new social ideals it expresses.

It seems that the new knowledge must inevitably act in the direction of diminishing the strength of the "Herd-instinct." The individual, released from the power of the Parent and Authority-complex, is far less likely to follow in blind obedience the dictates of the Community as a whole or the "Leaders" within it. Perhaps nothing is calculated to have greater consequences than this, for our present-day social system—above all, in the spheres of Morals, Politics, Economics—is crushed out of vitality between the millstones of the dominant so-called "leaders" on the one hand, and the mass, driven by unreasoning impulse for guidance, on the other. When the individual can place reliance on his own impulses (which is attainable to a far greater extent if he understands and faces them) and is no longer a prey to uncomprehended taboos and fears, he will be far less willing to subject himself to the crowd-impulses or to the guidance of "Authority." (For example, he will not be stampeded into anti-Alien legislation, terrified by "the German menace," or led by "fashion" to admire a futile, ill-considered type of education.) This mind-independence will go far to construct a Society which has a real function, in that it expresses and sums up the desires and opinions of the individual members who constitute it.

Moreover, the Community will achieve a greater fluidity in Law and Custom, in part for the reason cited above. In his Unconscious man looks upon Law and Custom as the voice of a dreaded and reverenced Authority—the Father re-incarnated—who may not be defied with impunity, however incomprehensible the dictates. He dare not bring his spontaneous impulses to bear upon this authority, hence in civilized society Custom and Law remain as a dead weight upon freedom of thought and action. In part for another reason this situation holds good. So strong is man's impulse towards certain activities, that only by the fear of heavy penalties imposed can he suppress those impulses which he both possesses and fears. The truth of this can be noted from such instances as our marriage and property Laws, many of our sexual customs, punishments for certain actions (e.g. for homosexual practices between adults), our would-be taboos concerning nearly all the bodily functions, and so on. Psycho-analytic research, by showing the immense variety and complexity of man's impulses and needs in all such directions, will prevent so deadening a crystallization of ideas, and will help us to realize that such impulses, however undesired, cannot disappear through repressive law and custom.

Not only will there be negative results—the removal of obstruction to freedom of development—but also positive ones. The energy formerly used up, both by the Individual on account of his Inhibitions and by the Community in preservation of its unnecessary Taboos, can be set free for purposes useful to both. In William Morris's *News from Nowhere* it will be remembered that the Buildings once occupied as prisons had become educational institutions, and the once gaolers were the Teachers and Advisers—a concrete illustration of the type of change which may be expected.

If it is objected that freedom for impulse will possibly bring disastrous results in its train, the answer must be, first, that impulse works in the direction of Sublimation as well as towards primitive wishes, and the human being needs to express the former just as much as the latter, possibly more so, provided he has some adequate fulfilment for the primitive impulses; secondly, that only by knowing and understanding where and how these latter lead can any control over them be obtained. The community wherein these impulses are merely suppressed and repressed is doing nothing to educate them and use them for its ultimate purposes.

The hypocrisy and sentimentality which overlays so much of our life, obscuring and distorting what is beneath, can be remedied to a great extent through more knowledge. In every community there are the people whose inhibitions are so strong that they cannot even glimpse the existing facts (akin to those remarkable Heads of Co-Education Schools who always blandly assure their audiences, "There are *no* Sex-problems in *our* schools"); there are others who see some of the facts, but turn away from them, usually maintaining that any investigation of what they call "dangerous" or "unpleasant" is calculated to bring still worse harm, or that such matters are for the expert only, or some similar rationalization of their own fear.

Few people are as sincere and intelligent in outlook as Robert Louis Stevenson, who wrote from Vailimá in 1894, in a letter to his cousin, R. A. M. Stevenson: "As I go on in life, day by day, I become more of a bewildered child; I cannot get used to this world, to procreation, to heredity, to sight and hearing. . . . The prim, obliterated, polite face of life, and the broad bawdy and orgiastic —or mænadic—foundations form a spectacle to which no habit reconciles me."

Stevenson here seems to have realized the facts of existence and his own problem in relation to them. It is possible that through Psycho-Analysis we may arrive at some path of reconciliation between the two extremes as felt by him, by ceasing to divorce so entirely the two aspects, rendering the one less "prim, obliterated, polite," and the other less terrific (as it is to many) through removal of unnecessary fears and taboos. If such a reconciliation cannot be achieved, then at least man must know it and be reconciled to non-reconciliation, subscribing to part, if not the whole, of Nietzsche's maxim: "Not only must the necessary be borne, and on no account concealed—all idealism is falsehood in the face of necessity—but it must also be *loved*" (*Ecce Homo*).

And here let it be noted that Freud's theory propounds no easy and absolute "solutions" of problems, nothing, in the words of William James, "to lie back and rest upon," no determined goal reached or reachable; it does, however, supply us, first and foremost, with *knowledge* of the psyche's problems and methods of obtaining that knowledge, and were its achievement no more than this it would still go far to revolutionize human thought and activity. But, as has been pointed out, it can also help to *solve* these problems, bringing extraordinary illumination to bear upon all kinds of hitherto non-comprehended matters in personal and general life.

In certain spheres, especially, the findings of Freud are very far-reaching, and may call for great modification of current ideas and customs—namely, in the spheres of Family-life, Child-training, and systematic Educational work.

"It is as a splendid exploratory enterprise that we recommend Psycho-Analysis in Child-study," say the two authors of the pamphlet already quoted[1] (*supra*, p. 83) and those who will embark on this enterprise will find that it offers results yet undreamt of. In the very early stages of child-rearing and training perhaps Psycho-Analysis would seem to have more to say on the important *negative* side of the problem of Education. Since the work of repression

[1] *The Conflicts in the Unconscious of the Child*, M. D. Eder and Edith Eder.

and the complex-forming capacity are both functioning in the individual from birth, it is clear that the Environment and Education (using the latter word in its widest sense) of the early years must be very important in influence (Freud holds that the first three or four years of life are of vital significance to the future psychic orientation). In these few years the first steps are being taken by the Ego in the process of adaptation to the outside world, in which process complex and delicate problems must be adjusted, and disharmonies must inevitably develop. The work of the educator or trainer during this period might be summed up as consisting in how to find out the best method of *avoiding undue and illegitimate repression and the creation of unresolved complexes.* The achievement of such an aim—or, indeed, of anything at all near it—necessitates wide and deep knowledge, much psychological understanding, much sincerity, and one is often amazed at the glibness with which parents and teachers (especially the latter) will claim complete and accurate knowledge of their children and pupils.

Dr. Ernest Jones' warning should be noted in this connexion : " When one hears a fond mother confidently assert that her child tells her everything there is in his mind, one may be perfectly certain that she is the victim of a gross illusion. Not only does the child from the tenderest years instinctively preserve his inmost thoughts from any adult, however dear, but he is both unable and unwilling to formulate many of them even to himself, and these are by no means the least important."[1]

The matter of *understanding* the situation as described in the above quotation is so important that a few more words must be given to it. It is inevitable that resistance between the child mind and the adult mind should exist, following on Freud's hypothesis of mind, and until this is realized the work of the Educator will proceed on ineffective lines. The psychic Censorship working in the child-mind operates to prevent many of his thoughts and feelings from becoming manifest; in addition, the external taboos, which so early he has to recognize, lead him to realize that much of his inmost thought and impulse is not suitable to the standards of the adults around him. To give but one instance of

[1] *The Unconscious Mental Life of the Child,* Ernest Jones.

this: Freud and his fellow-workers have found how usual an occurrence it is for the child of four or five years old to turn from his parents and pursue private speculations on subjects —sex is pre-eminently one of them—concerning which he has been denied information, or about which he may never yet have questioned his elders. Later, these speculations are most often forgotten, and " an appearance of innocence is thus produced, deceptive to both outsider and the child himself."

As to the adult, the difficulty for him in penetrating into the child's mind lies in the barrier that exists between his own Consciousness and his Unconscious (that is, between adult and infantile mind in one and the same personality); until this barrier is overcome it is impossible for an adult to have even the qualifications for seeing the child's mind as it really is—he does not want to see those things in the child which exist unrecognized in his own Unconscious.

" This is the final answer to those critics of psycho-analysis who maintain that they have assiduously studied the child's mind without being able to find in it the various characteristics and contents described by psycho-analysts. Of course, they are unable to do so, for the simple reason that they are unable to see what is in their own mind. Until a person has access to the recesses of his own mind he certainly will fail to penetrate to the recesses of another's mind, above all, to those of a child's." [1]

The problem, then, of how to avoid illegitimate Repression and the creation of unresolvable Complexes can only be dealt with by those who have some understanding of the psychic situation; even then the difficulties are manifold, and there is space to touch upon only two or three of the most significant.

First, there is the problem of the swiftness and abruptness of the Education-process—above all, in the early aspects of it—by which the newborn creature is adapted to the civilized environment it enters. It has already been noted how delicate a process is Sublimation, and how little we yet know of its possible extent and limitations. Nevertheless, we practically demand that every individual shall achieve, in about the same period of time, more or less the same degree of Sublimation

[1] *The Unconscious Mental Life of the Child,* Ernest Jones.

—a demand obviously impossible, productive of acute disharmonies to some of the individuals concerned.

When, therefore, we have enough knowledge to realize that we must cease fitting every human being into a stereotyped pattern suitable to the existing social fabric, we shall begin to train and educate on the right lines. Probably no method imaginable can make the adaptation-process anything but painful, complex, fraught with difficulty. What can be done is to help to make this process as satisfactorily achieved as may be. We can avoid too great *haste*; for instance, we are far too apt to be over-clean, over-nice, over-proper in regard to the behaviour of the very young, even to the extent of punishing, instead of understanding, what we call lapses in good and decent manners. We have to allow far more experiment in the psychic sphere, watching where and how the child's own primitive impulses lead it, not necessarily always suffering those impulses to dominate, but trying to understand their significance and import. (How many young children, one wonders, belonging to "respectably-brought-up" families, are ever allowed freely to play with actual dirt of any kind they spontaneously find, or fully express their interest in their own bodily functions ?) It may be this procedure will seem to delay the child's external development, that he will not, so readily and early, be able to take his place in adult life; but this is not necessarily a disadvantage. We do not yet know enough to lay down rules on such a matter. We do know that a strikingly large percentage of the educated civilized persons, moving about in normal polite society, are handicapped either with some form of neurotic trouble or with some physical ailment (or, at least, with lack of physical and mental vitality), which must surely be proof of failure in our system of upbringing and education.

So far, then, we see two aspects specially to be avoided in the early training-process—namely, Over-haste and undue Uniformity. It is true we offer much lip-service to the ideal of Freedom for the child, but it is doubtful if we go beyond that stage; and even if we were sincere in our protestations, it would be impossible to carry out the ideal without knowledge. The "Freedom" so often discussed by would-be reformers (Eugenists, Montessorians, and a host of others) is worthless, since based on an ignorance of the child's psychic situation with which they profess to deal, and, above all, of their own psyche.

A third essential in this work of early training is a willingness on the part of the educators to face all the implications of the situation. Those who start with presumptions and prejudices concerning child-nature will inevitably fail here; they will be unwilling to recognize some of the impulses in the child and fearful of gratifying its curiosities. The whole question of honest and informed enlightenment is here involved, especially in the realm of sex inquiries and sex-instruction. Freud believes that in this sphere probably the deepest and most harmful repressions are formed. The parents and educators are so unwilling and unable to give enlightenment; the whole subject, naturally of intense interest to every young child, becomes shameful, a thing unfit to talk about with respected and admired adults, and gets consciously suppressed and unconsciously repressed. A willingness on the part of the adults to answer all questions truthfully, to face the references and implications which will emerge, to make their own knowledge as adequate as possible—this will help to get rid of some of the shames, furtiveness, illusions connected with sex-ideas. At the same time we realize through Psycho-analysis that in this direction, above all others, no easy solution is to be found. To suppose (as so many well-intentioned, ignorant persons do) that by telling the child "all about" sex-matters, answering his questions, behaving sensibly and intelligently over sex-affairs, the problem thereby will be solved, is to be in the greatest error. It is the same erroneous attitude which has advocated giving sex-instruction in large classes in School, to children of various ages and stages of development ("just as you teach History or Arithmetic," as one naïve, well-known educationist put it recently). Such an idea assumes that there is only the conscious mind to be considered, rational and logical, whereas the profundities of sex and sex-emotions appertain primarily to the Unconscious. But knowledge can do something, perhaps much, in such directions as the prevention of premature sexual excitation; the making of physical functions as much as possible an ordinary recognized affair, not wrapt in mystery and shame; less setting up of fixed standards of conduct, irrespective of the child's own nature.

In relation to the first point mentioned

above—the prevention of premature sex-excitement—Psycho-Analysis has much guidance to give. The popular idea that the child under five or six is incapable of sex-feelings has been rendered invalid through Freud's research, and he has made clear that at a very early age the child can be sexually-excited in ways unthought of by parents and nurses. In consequence, it seems as if much more care must be taken to prevent the young child (even at the infant stage) from witnessing or hearing sexual incidents, such as he is bound to do if he sleeps in the parents' bedroom, or shares a bed with someone else, or shares in bathing, dressing and undressing with the opposite sex—a practice quite usual in the case of children under five or six.

Thus, those who rather pride themselves in "advanced" sex-views and great breadth of outlook will have much to learn from the study of Freud, along with those others who hold more narrow and conventional views.

It has been impossible to do more than barely touch upon one or two of the most significant matters regarding the influence of the Psycho-analytic findings in early training and environment. Much of the work to be accomplished in the future is difficult and delicate. Years of patient investigation will be needed before results can be widely attained; but, at all events, in the words of a well-known Psycho-Analyst, "the first thing we have to learn is to stop doing harm; then, perhaps, we may learn to do good."

If we turn to the sphere of Family-life, we shall find that here, again, Psycho-Analysis has much illumination to give. In Family-life, as Freud has shown, the primitive impulses have some of their earliest and deepest fulfilment, from which is created the psychic trend of the individual's after-life. The rôle of the parents is, in part, to help the Parent-complex in the child to a harmonious development, or, at least, to abstain as far as may be from promoting the conflict. So intense may be the Family-ties, whether in positive or negative form, that the individual cannot free himself again, from which will arise many of his psychic difficulties later on. The mother who has knowledge, far from fostering too-absorbing family-intimacies (it is often regarded as something noble to love one's family to the virtual exclusion of the rest of the world!), above all, the too-great devotion and lover-like attitude of a son, will endeavour to turn outwards the child's emotional activities, and to cultivate in him a more objective impersonal life. Both Father and Mother can do much to prevent a too close dependence on themselves; they can avoid lavishing love and recognition gained quite without effort on the child's part—a danger in one direction—or of withholding due affection and recognition—a danger in the opposite direction, leading to Suppression and Introversion. Concerning these two harmful attitudes, the Swiss Psycho-Analyst and Pastor, Dr. Oskar Pfister (in *The Psycho-Analytic Method*), says that probably the greater danger lies in the over-attachment and over-estimation towards the parents, whereby the individual remains throughout life the inferior and dependent, dreading, yet rejoicing in, authority. He writes: "If the emancipation from the parents in favour of higher considerations (once enjoined by Jesus) does not occur, Stagnation and Regression appear. Even the highly-talented Jews and Chinese remain dependent on the father for centuries, and experience an ossification of their culture."

For the parents (or those acting in their place) such efforts will involve sacrifice, both in the direction of giving and of receiving love and intimacy from the child. The passionate possessive love of parent for child must be recognized as, in part, a manifestation of intense egocentric desire. The mother seeks gratification and fulfilment for her own emotional desires through such relations with her child, without concern for the child's harmonious development, and Psycho-Analysis reveals her attitude in its true light, no longer as altruism alone. In the same way, relationships with brothers and sisters must be understood and readjusted, so that these ties may not serve as stumbling-blocks in the path of adult development and independence. There are cases of brothers whose devotion (regarded as beautiful in the family-circle) to a sister is so intense that no other woman, throughout life, can displace the sister-image, and new ties (such as marriage, for example) become difficult or impossible. Similarly with a sister's fixation on a brother, or even in the case of a sister and sister, brother and brother attachment. Again, the relations between the parents themselves will be of immense influence in causing a reaction on their part towards the children. Freud has related the case of one of his patients, a woman, who was dominated by an anxiety-neurosis on account of her seven-year-old child, resulting in an absurdly excessive cossetting and worrying over every detail of the unfortunate child's existence. His health, his education, his clothes, his games—all were of the most terrible and painful importance to her. Analysis discovered that the mother was dissatisfied with her sexual and emotional life, was filled with self-reproach for her ungrateful attitude to her husband, and compensated for this (only known to her Unconscious) by an excessive zeal for her child's welfare, for whom, unconsciously, aversion was mingled with her conscious affection.

In the later stages of the child's development, where we reach Education in the formal and specific sense, Psycho-Analysis can give guidance and information of a more *positive* nature. Its function might be summed up as aiding us to discover: *How best to help and guide the sublimating capacity of the individual into channels most desirable and useful for himself and Society.*

In such work, clearly, the Teacher is bound to play a large part, and positively rather than negatively, since from the age of nine, often to that of eighteen or twenty, formal education in School and College is one of the biggest influences in the human being's life in modern times.

I can do no better than quote Freud's own words in respect to this matter: "Education can be described as incitement to the mastering of the Pleasure-principle, and to the replacement of this principle by the Reality-principle, and it will thus afford an aid to the process of development of the Ego, to this end making use of the premiums of love on the side of the Educators, and hence miscarrying when the spoiled child thinks that it already possesses this love regardless of effort." It seems likely that a great field of work will lie open, in the near future, for the educator who has studied Freud's theories and can apply them to his own line of work, perhaps even more possibilities for him than for the Physician, since his sphere is a wider one.

In his Introduction to *The Psycho-Analytic Method*, by Pfister, Freud expresses the view that there are to be expected very great results from the work of the Analyst-Educator in the future, who is in many respects, he holds, more suited to the application of Psycho-analytic principles in a general way than the Physician himself; and another Analyst, Riklin, of Zürich, says: "Obviously, we must greet the collaboration of Philologists, Pedagogues, and others with joy. We need them, and have the greatest stimulus to expect from them. For Psycho-Analysis can never be limited to Pathology. It is very desirable that the educated world should acquire psycho-analytic knowledge. It will then be less possible for the conflicts to hide behind the poor masks of the neuroses. A number of conflicts, then (for example, those of Puberty), will be judged quite differently, and will be led to Rational Solutions."

The Teacher with such knowledge will aim at a different goal, and seek to achieve that goal by methods different from current ones. His goal, to put it very briefly, will be to afford adequate outlets for necessary sublimation, to avoid "short cuts" to sublimation (which tend to create complexes), to aid the pupil to self-recognition, and to liberate mental energy as far as may be. These will be his objects rather than the setting up of standards (of life, thought, morals, etc.), or the impregnation of the pupils with any set of ideas from outside.

As to changed methods, the first important idea to grasp is that the Analyst-Educator will turn his attention to, and make use of, the Unconscious as well as the Conscious, a change which by itself would revolutionize our present educational system.

Probably one of the commonest and worst effects of the latter is the disintegration of the psyche which it creates. The Unconscious, left untouched, often for the whole of scholastic life, by the direct education carried on day by day, is split off from the Conscious and cannot get linked on again.

We see this process before our eyes, first in the obvious manifest result which divorces "school life" from the rest of the child's life, creating two watertight compartments wherein he lives and moves at different times and places, the gulf between the two unbridged. No one has expressed this anomaly better than Mr. Wells in various of his writings—above all, in *The New Macchiavelli* (that wonderful Chapter "Scholastic" should be read by all who are interested in the subject), and in his last book, *The Undying Fire.* He has put the matter in a nutshell: "Here all about me was London, a vast inexplicable being, a vortex of gigantic forces, that filled and overwhelmed me with impressions, that stirred my imagination to a perpetual vague enquiry; and my school not only offered no key to it, but had practically no comment to make upon it at all." [1]

But this divorce of interests and environments, largely a conscious process, is a far less harmful matter than the psychic disintegration which goes on under our present system. This latter brings about the Fantasying which creates a perpetual gulf between Conscious and Unconscious, preventing the former from being illumined by the latter. The child, using only its Consciousness for its educational work, withdraws for its pleasure and gratification into the Unconscious, which need play no part in the conscious intellectual life. This, again, perpetuates infantile thinking (since no relationship need be effected between the primitive Unconscious and the more developed Consciousness), which, in its turn, makes ever more difficult all abstract thinking. Thus it is we can produce individuals, the products of a most "advanced" "intellectual" educational system, who yet remain infantile and regressive in their inmost selves—above all, in methods of thinking and feeling. I have an instance of this in mind to serve as an illustration: A woman of my acquaintance, accepted as highly intellectual

[1] *The New Macchiavelli*, ch. 5.

in her circle, has told me of her incapability for, and aversion to, abstract thought, even of the simplest kind; yet in her school and college career she carried off every Prize and Distinction owing to an extraordinarily quick mind-receptivity, excellent memory, and general swiftness of thought in a superficial sense. But through all the years of her formal education, as she has told me with bitterness, there was no cultivation of the deeper mind-stuff, no knowledge displayed by the teachers as to what was going on, no measures taken to bring her back from perpetual fantasy-making of an infantile character, which characteristic, at the age of fifty, still has her in thrall.

With such considerations in mind, the questions of memory-work, choice of subjects, relation between so-called "intellectual" and emotional results of education, and a host of others, must be treated from very different standpoints than the current ones. Perhaps an even more difficult matter, and one likely to be more influenced by Psycho-Analysis than the problems already cited, is the Teacher and his function.

The Teacher is the Father or Mother-substitute, hence all the difficulties which arise from the Parent-relation must be involved in his relations with his pupil, plus the problems of his own personal relationship.

So the Teacher has to face all the difficult questions of Authority, Indulgence, Equality, Freedom, Emotional Relationships from a new point of view—the standpoint of the Unconscious as well as the Conscious. To discuss this in detail here is impossible, owing to limitations of space, but a word or two may indicate what is meant. The Teacher who exercises, successfully perhaps, great authority over his pupils, must learn to see what that authority implies and what result it is producing. It may be that an excessive father-complex in himself (an intense reaction against the father) has produced his love of exercising authority—a bad thing in so far as it is a false and not understood reaction. Further, his exercise of authority, so willingly and reverentially accepted by the pupils, may be merely storing up a harvest of evil for the latter, by creating a too-excessive father-complex in them, which ultimately will have *its* reaction. Similarly the desire for equality with the pupils, or even for a kind of subjection to them (quite common among would-be educational reformers), is a symptom of masochistic pleasure—a delight in inferiority and suffering—which certainly is not to be hailed as any benefit either to teacher or pupils. The attitude towards Punishment, again, of whatever type, may be very significant and revealing, if investigated psycho-analytically. The teacher who "believes in punishment" may come to find that in this belief he is merely expressing his own sadistic impulses, unrecognized by himself, and that by inflicting punishment he is helping to build up in the pupil a like sexual-sadistic trend (recalling Rousseau's experiences of corporal punishment).

In short, without an understanding of his own Unconscious to some fair extent, it will be impossible for the Teacher to know *why* he is acting in certain directions, or *what effects* his action has in the very important sphere of unconscious psychic life—hence in the sphere, ultimately, of Consciousness. And the result will be what we see to-day—confusion and futility throughout our educational system. This is the opinion, expressed in gentle terms by Pfister: "As often as I had the pleasure of analysing professional colleagues, I experienced a profound shock upon the recognition of manifold educational mistakes which had been committed under the influence of complexes."

So cursory a survey of the results of Psycho-analytic knowledge upon Education can do no justice to the subject, only the fringe of which has been touched. But it will surely be obvious to all who think that there are bound to be results, profound and significant, in the Educational sphere, just as in those others already noted—the spheres of Individual, Social, and National life.

It is, therefore, as a revelation of new knowledge foreshadowing the most hopeful possibilities, and as an instrument potent for sounding the yet unplumbed sea of mind, that Psycho-Analysis claims our interest and our study.

For those even who are uneasy before its revelations and dispute its findings, investigation may prove fruitful. If convinced opponents must still continue to exist, may they be opponents in the spirit of Voltaire, who wrote to his arch-enemy Helvetius: "I wholly disapprove of what you say—and will defend to the death your right to say it."

APPENDIX

DURING the last five or six years Professor Freud has continuously carried on his researches and has elaborated to a far greater extent some of his earlier work, carrying into new spheres some of the theories already established, and forming additional theories in regard to certain problems, though without negating any of his fundamental conceptions.

It seems desirable, therefore, with the present issue of this volume (first published in April 1920) to draw attention to some of the most important developments in the work of Freud (and of his followers), although the limited space available will allow of nothing more than mere mention.

The conception of *Narcissism* (that is, that state in which self becomes the love-object and the libido is inhibited to a marked degree from turning towards external objects) is now held by Freud as an essential and important stage in sexual development occurring between the earlier auto-erotic and the later object-love stages, and bearing a close relationship to homo-sexuality. The evolution of Narcissism in the individual, its bearing on the psychology of love, its relation to sublimation, and to certain neuroses—these and other aspects have all been investigated by Freud in a series of essays, and the conclusions he makes shed much new light on psychic development as a whole.

Metapsychology, which he has been considering for the last few years, is the term applied by him "*to denote a psychology which will regard every mental process from three points of view; namely, the dynamic, the topographical, and the economical.*"[1] Very briefly to explain the foregoing, it may be said that Freud is here stressing three aspects of mental phenomena: in the first place, the *dynamics* of the mechanism which produces them; in the second place, the *regions of the mind* in which mental processes occur and the relationship of these to one another (such as, in consciousness, in the preconscious, in the unconscious); in the third place, *the laws of production, distribution and consumption* of psychical energy according to the principle of obtaining the greatest advantage for the ego with the least effort.

Profound and complex ideas have been expounded by Freud in one of his recent books now issued in an English Translation (published by the International Psycho-Analytical Press, 1922) entitled *Beyond the Pleasure Principle.* Here he deals with the relation of ego-impulses and death-impulses, and questions whether

[1] From a lecture delivered before the Medical Section of the British Psychological Society by Dr. Ernest Jones (January, 1920).

there may not be a more primitive and more dominating force than the Pleasure-principle itself, namely, a *Repetition-compulsion*. By this he signifies a powerful compulsion towards certain behaviour or mental attitudes which "gives the impression of a pursuing fate, a dæmonic trait in the destiny. . . . Thus one knows people with whom every human relationship ends in the same way: benefactors whose protégés . . . invariably after a time desert them in ill-will: . . . men with whom every friendship ends in the friend's treachery . . . lovers whose tender relationships with women each and all run through the same phases and come to the same end, and so on.[1]

In *Group Psychology and the Analysis of the Ego* (International Psycho-Analytical Press, 1922) Freud has made a new incursion into Sociology. In this work he points out that the sharp distinctions, so attractive to certain popular sociologists, between the psychology of the individual and that of the group are not substantiated, or at least need careful examination. The individual has from the very earliest to adapt himself to a group: the relationship of the child to the family is the prototype of that of the adult to society. He especially draws attention to the reaction of the crowd or group to its leaders, and from this standpoint he analyses two artificial groups, the Church and the Army, bringing to bear upon these the knowledge already obtained from Psycho-analysis. In the Church the individual comes to identify himself with Christ, to love his fellows as Christ loves them. The soldier takes his Army-leaders as his ideal whilst identifying himself with his comrades. A primary group or crowd may be defined as a number of individuals who have replaced their particular ego-ideals by an object in common and have identified themselves in their own ego with one another. Whilst the libido which wields groups together cannot properly be called homo- or hetero-sexual, it is of importance to recognize that homo-sexuality comports far better with group relationships. The phenomena of hypnotism, of the neuroses, and the study of primitive man are touched upon to throw light on the obscurities of crowd-psychology.

The above slight survey of the more recent work will, it is hoped, give a small idea of the immense avenues of research being opened up, and will indicate the new directions in which Freud is projecting his thought.

B. L.

December 1922.

[1] *Beyond the Pleasure Principle*, pp. 22 and 23.

WORKS OF REFERENCE IN ENGLISH

ABRAHAM, K.

Dreams and Myths (1913). (*Nervous and Mental Disease, Monograph Series, No.* 15.)

BRILL, A. A.

Psychoanalysis—Its Theory and Practical Application. (2nd Edition, 1914.)

CORIAT, I.

The Meaning of Dreams (1915).

EDER, M. D.

War Shock. The Psycho-Neuroses in War Psychology and Treatment (1917).

EDER, M. D., AND EDER, EDITH.

The Conflicts in the Unconscious of the Child. (Reprinted from *Child Study,* 1917.)

FERENCZI, S.

Contributions to Psycho-Analysis. (Auth. Translation by Ernest Jones, 1916.)

*FLUGEL, J. C.

The Psycho-Analytic Study of the Family (1921). (The International Psycho-Analytical Press.)

FORSYTH, DAVID.

The Technique of Psycho-Analysis. (Kegan Paul, 1922.)

FREUD, S.

Selected Papers on Hysteria. (Auth. Translation by A. A. Brill, 1909.)

Three Contributions to the Sexual Theory. (Auth. Translation by A. A. Brill, 1910.)

The Interpretation of Dreams. (Auth. Translation by A. A. Brill, 1913.)

The Psychopathology of Everyday Life. (Auth. Translation by A. A. Brill, 1914.)

On Dreams. (Auth. Translation by M. D. Eder, 1914.)

Wit and its Relation to the Unconscious. (Auth. Translation by A. A. Brill, 1916.)

Totem and Tabu. (Auth. Translation by A. A. Brill, 1918.)

Delusion and Dream. (Translation by Helen Downey, 1919.)

**Introductory Lectures on Psycho-Analysis* (1920). (The International Psycho-Analytical Press.)

**Beyond the Pleasure-Principle.* (Auth. Translation from the Second German Edition by C. J. M. Hubback, 1922.) (The International Psycho-Analytical Press.)

Appendix

FREUD, S. (*continued.*)

**Group Psychology and the Analysis of the Ego.* (Auth. Translation from the German by James Strachey, 1922.) (The International Psycho-Analytical Press.)

FRINK, H. W.

Morbid Fears and Compulsions (1918).

HITSCHMANN, E.

Freud's Theory of the Neuroses. (*Nervous and Mental Diseases, Monograph Series,* 1913.)

HOLT, E.

The Freudian Wish and its Place in Ethics (1915).

JONES, ERNEST.

Papers on Psycho-Analysis. (Revised and Enlarged Edition, 1918.)

The Psychology of Everyday Life. (Reprinted from *American Journal of Psychology,* October, 1911, Vol. 22.)

The Unconscious Mental Life of the Child. (Reprinted from *Child Study,* April, 1916.)

The Œdipus-Complex as an Explanation of Hamlet's Mystery (1910).

**Psycho-Analysis and the War-Neuroses.* (Drs. Jones, Abraham, Ferenczi, Simmel (1921). (The International Psycho-Analytical Press.)

**Essays in Applied Psycho-Analysis* (Ready shortly.) (The International Psycho-Analytical Press.)

JUNG, C. G.

Studies in Word-Association. (Auth. Translation by M. D. Eder, 1918.)

Collected Papers on Analytical Psychology (1916).

The Psychology of the Unconscious (1916).

LAY, W.

Man's Unconscious Conflict (1918).

The Child's Unconscious Mind (1919).

LOW, BARBARA.

Psycho-Analysis and Education. (Ready shortly.) (Kegan Paul.)

MACCURDY.

War Neuroses (1918).

MITCHELL, T. W.

The Psychology of Medicine. (Methuen, 1922.)

An Outline of Psycho-Analysis

PAUL, EDEN AND CEDAR.
Translators of *The Diary of a Young Girl* (1920). (Introduction by Freud.)

PFISTER, O.
The Psycho-Analytic Method. (Translation by D. C. Payne, 1917.)
Psycho-Analysis in the Service of Education. (Auth. Translation. Henry Kimpton, London, 1922.)
Expressionism in Art. (Auth. Translation from the German by Barbara Low and M. Mügge.) (Kegan Paul, 1922.)

PUTNAM, J. J.
Human Motives (1915).
**Essays in Psycho-Analysis* (1921). (The International Psycho-Analytical Press.)

RANK, O.
The Myth of the Birth of the Hero. (*Nervous and Mental Disease, Monograph Series, No.* 18.)

RANK, O., AND SACHS, H.
The Significance of Psycho-Analysis for the Mental Sciences. (Translated by Smith Ely Jelliffe, *Nervous and Mental Disease, Monograph Series, No.* 23.)

RIKLIN, F.
Wish Fulfilment and Fairy Tales. (Translation by Smith Ely Jelliffe, *Monograph Series.*)

RIVERS, W. H. R.
Dreams and Primitive Culture.

SILBERER, H.
Problems of Mysticism and its Symbolism. (Translation by Smith Ely Jelliffe, 1917.)

VARENDONCK, J.
The Psychology of Day-Dreams (1920). (Introduction by Freud.)

WHITE, W.
Mechanisms of Character Formation (1916).
